jB   Lisandrelli, Elaine
ANGELOU   Slivinski.

            Maya Angelou.

$17.95

DATE		

—African-American Biographies—

MAYA ANGELOU
More Than a Poet

Series Consultant:
Dr. Russell L. Adams, Chairman
Department of Afro-American Studies, Howard University

Elaine Slivinski Lisandrelli

ENSLOW PUBLISHERS, INC.

44 Fadem Road   P.O. Box 38
Box 699   Aldershot
Springfield, N.J. 07081   Hants GU12 6BP
U.S.A.   U.K.

For my parents, Leo and Gabriella Slivinski, with love

Library of Congress Cataloging-in-Publication Data

Lisandrelli, Elaine Slivinski.
  Maya Angelou: more than a poet / Elaine Slivinski Lisandrelli.
    p. cm. — (African-American biographies)
  Includes bibliographical references and index.
  Summary: Portrays the life of this multi-faceted African-American poet,
author, and educator.
  ISBN 0-89490-684-4
  1. Angelou, Maya—Biography—Juvenile literature. 2. Afro-American
women authors—20th century—Biography—Juvenile literature.
3. Afro-American entertainers—United States—Biography—Juvenile
literature. 4. Civil rights workers—United States—Biography—Juvenile
literature. 5. Women entertainers—United States—Biography—Juvenile
literature. [1. Angelou, Maya. 2. Afro-Americans—Biography.
3.Women—Biography.] I. Title. II. Series.
PS3551.N464Z75 1996
818'.5409—dc20   95-35212
[B]   CIP
                                                              AC
Printed in the United States of America

10 9 8 7 6 5 4 3 2 1

Illustration Credits:
Charles Simmons, p. 110; Courtesy of the Rockefeller Foundation, p. 98; David
Pharr Collection, p. 47; George Washington High School, San Francisco, pp. 40,
42; Mary Ellen Mark/Library, pp. 8, 59, 61, 88; National Archives, pp. 31, 70;
Photofest, p. 17; Photographs and Prints Division, Schomburg Center for
Research in Black Culture, The New York Public Library, Astor, Lenox and
Tilden Foundations, pp. 96, 101; Ted Pontiflet, c/o P.S. Gibson, 400 West 43rd.
St., New York, NY, 10036, pp. 91, 105, 107; University of Massachusetts,
Amherst, p. 81; The White House, pp. 10, 12. 111.

Cover Illustration: The White House

**Excerpts from the following works are reprinted by permission of Random
House, Inc.:**
I KNOW WHY THE CAGED BIRD SINGS by Maya Angelou, Copyright ©1969 by
Maya Angelou; "ON THE PULSE OF MORNING" by Maya Angelou, Copyright
©1993 by Maya Angelou; *AND STILL I RISE* by Maya Angelou, Copyright ©1978
by Maya Angelou; *GATHER TOGETHER IN MY NAME* by Maya Angelou,
Copyright ©1974 by Maya Angelou; *THE HEART OF A WOMAN* by Maya
Angelou, Copyright ©1981 by Maya Angelou.

Contents

1

"THE PULSE OF
MORNING"

n a country store in the dusty town of Stamps,
Arkansas, a young girl sits near the candy
counter. Outside, a sharp wind rustles
through the shingles, but inside a potbellied stove
warms the small store. Between customers she often
writes poetry or reads from her beloved books.[1] These
pursuits take her mind off the pain of growing up in
the segregated South of the 1930s, where opportunities are denied to her because she is African
American. On this day she memorizes the Presidents
of the United States in chronological order.[2]

A tap on the counter disturbs her concentration. She never intended to ignore the customer who came to patronize her grandmother's store.[3] With a sigh, she closes the book. She accurately scoops up a half-pound of flour, and gently places it into a thin paper sack.[4]

◆◆◆◆

Years later, after she journeyed far away from this Arkansas town, and overcame many hardships, a special opportunity was presented to this child who grew up to be Maya Angelou—author, playwright, professional stage and screen producer, director, performer, and singer. On a November day in 1992, the future forty-second President of the United States, William Jefferson Clinton, invited Angelou to compose and deliver a poem for his Inauguration Day ceremony. Her talent earned her the distinction of being the first African American and the first woman in the history of our nation to do so.

Maya Angelou felt grateful.[5] No poet had partici-pated in a presidential inauguration swearing-in ceremony since 1961, when Robert Frost read his work at President Kennedy's inauguration. But Angelou was terrified, too.[6] Creating a poem that must touch the hearts of millions is a difficult task. Throughout her sixty-four years, Angelou had encountered many difficult tasks, and each time she embraced the challenge as an opportunity.

In preparation, Angelou spent weeks reading the works of scholar W.E.B. DuBois, abolitionist Frederick Douglass, poet Frances Ellen Watkins Harper, and sermons of African-American preachers. Often she left her beautiful home in Winston-Salem, North Carolina, and checked into a quiet hotel room to write. With her Bible, dictionary, and thesaurus by her side, she wrote and rewrote the poem on yellow legal pads, soon filling two hundred pages. As she searched for more ideas and reflected upon what she had already written, she played a game of solitaire.

Between her writing sessions, people asked about her progress and suggested topics she should address. Angelou remembers, "Even on an airplane, people would pass by my seat and say: 'Mornin,' finish your poem yet?'"[7]

Angelou kept writing. The themes she longed to impress upon the nation—that we human beings "are more alike than unalike"[8] and that "we may encounter many defeats but we must not be defeated,"[9] flowed through the 668 well-chosen words of the poem she called "On the Pulse of Morning."

The delivery of the poem was crucial, too. Bertha Flowers, a special woman from Angelou's past, had once told Angelou, "Words mean more than what is set down on paper. It takes the human voice to infuse them with the shades of deeper meaning."[10] And on that cold Inauguration Day of January 20, 1993, Angelou

Solitaire keeps Maya Angelou's hands busy while she is thinking.

took her carefully crafted poem and eloquently gave meaning to her written words.

After being introduced to the audience as a "noted educator, historian, and author," Maya Angelou began with images that would speak throughout the poem:

> *A Rock, a River, a Tree*
> *Hosts to species long since departed*[11]

The January sun reflected off her hoop earrings and the metal buttons of her navy blue coat. Her deep, rich voice, once described as "the sound of summer evening thunder rumbling somewhere off in the distance,"[12] gave power to the alliterations of "distant destiny," "Marked the mastodon," and "wall of the world."[13] Maya Angelou's vision of each of us as a "descendant of some passed-on traveler"[14] reminded many of the suffering of those who came to this country, "arriving on a nightmare,/Praying for a dream."[15]

She encouraged us to have hope for the future even though our past has been troubled.

> *History, despite its wrenching pain,*
> *Cannot be unlived, but if faced*
> *With courage, need not be lived again.*[16]

Millions across the nation listened to their radios or watched as TV cameras focused on the faces in the crowd whose differences in race, color, creed, profession, and persuasion make up our nation. Tears filled some eyes. To each listener, Angelou seemed to speak personally.

□□□

Maya Angelou delivers her inspirational poem at the Presidential
Inauguration of William Jefferson Clinton on January 20, 1993.

Lift up your eyes
Upon this day breaking for you.
Give birth again
To the dream.[17]

The television camera captured President Clinton smiling and nodding approvingly at these lines:

Here, on the pulse of this fine day,
You may have the courage
To look up and out and upon me,
The Rock, the River, the Tree, your country.
No less to Midas than the mendicant.
No less to you now than the mastodon then.[18]

Novelist Louise Erdrich praised Angelou's forceful delivery. "Her presence was so powerful and momentous, she made a statement that I was personally longing to see and hear."[19]

Here, on the pulse of this new day,
You may have the grace to look up and out
and into your sister's eyes,
And into your brother's face,
Your country,
And say simply
Very simply
With hope—
Good morning.[20]

As Maya Angelou concluded her poem, loud cheers, enthusiastic applause, a standing ovation, and

Maya Angelou meets with President Clinton again, several months after the inauguration.

a hug by the new President greeted her. "I loved your poem," President Clinton remarked, and he promised to hang a copy in the White House.[21] Television news correspondent Peter Jennings referred to Maya Angelou's poem as her "vision of America."[22]

This poem that "electrified the nation"[23] symbolized the hope President Clinton wanted to instill in the country—the hope that one person can overcome hardships and injustices and still look at the world with love and forgiveness.

She once told television journalist Bill Moyers, "You can never leave home. You take it with you wherever you go."[24] Maya Angelou's vision of America, first formed in Stamps, Arkansas, had come with her to Washington, D.C., in the form of a poem.

Many who listened to her eloquence that historic day did not realize that she had endured a long and often painful journey to arrive at this shining moment.

2

THE CAGED BIRD

aya Angelou, born Marguerite Johnson on April 4, 1928, experienced her first significant journey when she was three years old. After her parents' divorce, she and her four-year-old brother, Bailey Johnson, Jr., traveled by train from Long Beach, California, to Stamps, Arkansas. It was Bailey who had given Marguerite her name when he refused to call her Marguerite, but addressed her as Mya Sister, then My, and finally Maya.

On their long journey, Maya's and Bailey's tickets were pinned to Bailey's inside coat pocket. Name tags attached to their wrists bore the words, "To Whom It May Concern." No adults accompanied them, but in the 1930s it was not uncommon for young African-American children to travel back and forth between parents and grandparents as parents tried to create a better life for themselves away from the South. A porter was assigned to look out for Maya and Bailey, but he got off the train in Arizona, leaving the two small travelers to be cared for by other passengers on the train.

In Stamps, Arkansas, a poor town that knew droughts, floods, and lynchings, Maya and Bailey met their father's mother, Mrs. Annie Henderson. She had remarried after Maya and Bailey's grandfather, William Johnson, left her, around the turn of the twentieth century, with two small sons to raise. Annie Henderson was a tall, powerful, hard-working, and courageous woman who never failed to thank God for letting her see another day.

Bailey and Maya soon began calling her Momma. Momma cooked delicious meals and sewed their clothes. Maya remembered that she and Bailey "looked like walking wallpaper—all our clothes were made out of the same material."[1] Momma insisted that they obey her two commandments: Always be clean and always be respectful. These rules were not always easy to follow. Being clean meant going outside in the icy cold winter and washing up by the well before going to bed. Being respectful meant remembering that "all adults had to be addressed as Mister, Missus, Miss, Auntie, Cousin, Unk, Uncle, Buhbah, Sister, Brother, and a thousand other appellations indicating familial relationship and the lowliness of the addresser."[2] But Maya and Bailey loved Momma and tried to obey.

Momma owned the William Johnson General Merchandise Store. Built at the beginning of the 1900s in the heart of the African-American section of Stamps, Arkansas, it housed a variety of goods: canned pineapple, cheese, soda crackers, oranges, silver-wrapped chocolate kisses, mash for hogs, corn for chickens, flower seeds, and shoestrings. The Store, always spoken of with a capital S, was Maya's favorite place:[3]

> I remember the wonderful smells: the aroma of the pickle barrel, the bulging sacks of corn, the luscious ripe fruit. You could pick up a can of snuff from North Carolina, a box of matches from Ohio, a yard of ribbon from New York. All of those places seemed terribly exotic to me. I would fantasize how people from there had actually touched those objects. It was a magnificent experience![4]

Maya also had the family love of her Uncle Willie, her father's brother, who had been crippled by a childhood accident. Although the right side of his body was severely paralyzed, his left hand and arm were large and powerful. He was a proud and sensitive man who lovingly looked after Maya and Bailey as if they were his own.

Esther Rolle played Mrs. Annie Henderson and Constance Good played young Maya in the Store scene from the television adaptation of Angelou's autobiography, *I Know Why the Caged Bird Sings.*

Momma's and Uncle Willie's love surrounded Maya and Bailey, but their love could not protect them from hatred and fear in the segregated South. Even though slavery had ended, some whites continued to mistreat blacks. Members of the Ku Klux Klan (KKK) burned large crosses and beat, lynched, or tortured blacks just because of the color of their skin. Blacks had to use separate entrances at movie theaters, drink from separate water fountains, and sit in the backs of buses. They were also denied jobs and opportunities.

Maya dreamed of having long blond hair and light blue eyes so she could look like "one of the sweet little white girls who were everybody's dream of what was right with the world."[5] Maya was sure that a cruel fairy stepmother, jealous of her beauty, had turned Maya into "a too-big Negro girl, with nappy black hair, broad feet and a space between her teeth that would hold a number two pencil."[6]

Whenever she and Bailey crossed the railroad tracks that divided Stamps into two sections, white and black, they felt like "explorers walking without weapons into man-eating animals' territory."[7] Once, on this journey, Maya had fantasized that suddenly she would be white and "wouldn't be looked at with such loathing."[8] But the magic did not happen; so she held her head high, gritted her teeth, and courageously walked into the white section of Stamps.

Some poor white children who lived on their grandmother's land often ordered Uncle Willie around the Store and insulted her grandmother. Maya survived the humiliation, but the scars still remain.

In Stamps Maya witnessed others beaten down by life. At dusk, when the cotton truck dropped off the workers, Maya saw evidence of their difficult day. Their backs and shoulders were slumped over. Their hands and feet had become swollen and the cotton bolls had cut their fingers. Memories of scenes like this helped forge Maya's compassion.

There were also quiet times in Stamps when brother and sister developed a special relationship. They played Hide and Seek and Follow the Leader and talked to each other in pig Latin.

Bailey and Maya attended the Lafayette County Training School, which was perched on a dirt hill. Unlike the white school in Stamps, their school was not decorated by lawns, hedges, climbing ivy, or tennis courts. At the black school, the only "extra" was a rusty hoop for basketball. Their black teachers were not paid the same salaries that white teachers received. Despite these poor conditions, Bailey and Maya learned to rattle off their multiplication tables, and they loved to read books.[9]

After school, Maya and Bailey helped out at the Store and completed their evening chores. They gave scoops of corn to the chickens and made a slop of sour dry mash, leftover food, and oily dishwater for the hogs. Before Maya and Bailey went to bed, Momma and Uncle Willie made sure their homework was done, their prayers said, and their feet washed.

Church, the central meeting place for African Americans, also provided an escape from the hate of segregation and a sense of belonging to a community. Momma and her grandchildren spent a lot of time there:

> We went to church all day Sunday. Then on Monday evening we went to missionary meetings. Tuesday evening, usher boy meetings. Wednesday evening, prayer meeting. Thursday evening, choir practice. We went to church all the time and at all those meetings we sang.[10]

Maya loved the sermons and the African-American spirituals, "folk songs that cried out against the painful cruelty of slavery, expressed faith in the hope of freedom in the next life if not this one, and appealed to God for succor."[11] She later recognized the lasting influence their words and melodies had on her writing. "Actually, the first poetry I ever knew was the poetry of the gospel songs and the spirituals."[12]

In her early years in Stamps, Maya thought that both her parents, Bailey Johnson, Sr., and Vivian Baxter Johnson, were dead. This perception was shattered one Christmas, when presents arrived from her parents, who lived separately in "a heaven called California." Maya's gifts of her father's photograph, a tea set, and a blonde-haired doll with blue eyes and rosy cheeks brought tears and painful questions for her. Why had their parents sent them away? What had they done that was so terrible? Momma scolded them for being ungrateful: "You think your momma and poppa went to all the trouble to send you these nice play pretties to make you go out in the cold and cry?"[13] Maya and Bailey hid the visible signs of hurt, but their emotional pain still lingered.

A year later, Maya's father, Bailey Johnson, Sr., a doorman at a beautiful hotel in Santa Monica, California, arrived in Stamps, and as Maya recalled, "my seven-year-old world humpty-dumptied, never to be put back together again."[14]

After spending several weeks in Stamps, Maya's father announced that he was taking the children to California. Bailey was excited, but Maya was torn. She did not want to be without Bailey, but she did not want to leave Momma either. She thought about drowning herself in the pond to end her dilemma. Momma masked her sadness by making new clothes for Maya's journey. Her parting words to Maya were, "You be a good girl now. You hear? Don't you make people think I didn't raise you right. You hear?"[15] She packed fried chicken and sweet potato pie in Daddy Bailey's gray car, which already was filled with his leather suitcases and Maya's and Bailey's cardboard boxes.

During the trip, Bailey and Daddy Bailey joked and laughed, while Maya sat in the back. Every now and then Maya heard, "Are you comfortable back there, Daddy's baby?"[16] Soon her father announced a new destination—St. Louis, Missouri—the city where their mother now lived. Bailey was in shock, and Maya cried at this surprise turn of events.[17]

When they met their mother, whose red-lipped smile lit up the room, Bailey fell instantly in love.[18] Maya was mesmerized, for she had "never seen a woman as pretty as she who was called 'Mother.'"[19] Vivian Baxter Johnson was a kind, fun-loving, well-educated woman who was trained as a nurse but who did not work in that profession until years later. Within a few days, their father was on his way back to California alone. Maya remembered, "He was a stranger, and if he chose to leave us with a stranger, it was all of one piece."[20]

To the children from Stamps, who had used out-houses and listened to the rustle of chinaberry trees in the warm Arkansas breeze, St. Louis in the mid-1930s seemed like another country. Here doorbells, flushing toilets, and the noise of cars, trains, and buses were familiar sounds. In this city Maya learned to eat thin-sliced ham, jelly beans mixed with peanuts, and lettuce on sandwiches.

While Mother Dear, as Bailey often referred to her, was preparing a place for them, the children lived with their Grandmother and Grandfather Baxter in a big house on Caroline Street for six months. The Baxters, she learned, were loyal to one another, and her uncles had bad tempers and a reputation for taking the law into their own hands.

Before moving in with their mother and her mother's boyfriend, known to the children only as Mr. Freeman, Maya and Bailey often met their Mother Dear at Louie's Bar. In the smoke-filled room, Maya and Bailey sipped on soft drinks, enjoyed boiled shrimp, and learned how to dance the Time Step, a series of taps, jumps, and rests that required expert coordination.

In St. Louis they attended Toussaint L'Ouverture Grammar School. Maya and Bailey were far ahead of the city children, because they read books constantly and had received excellent math training from working at the Store in Stamps. Each skipped a grade. Maya got her first library card and spent most of her Saturdays at the library.

During the winter, she and Bailey filled a bowl with snow, poured canned milk and sugar over it, and made ice cream. Evenings were spent doing supper dishes, completing homework, reading, playing games like Monopoly™, or listening to *The Lone Ranger*, *Crime Busters*, or *The Shadow* on the radio.

Horrifying nightmares often awakened Maya. They seemed to be created by the scary stories she read,[21] her vivid imagination, and memories of her hectic life.[22] When the nightmares were especially bad, Mother Dear took Maya to sleep with her and Mr. Freeman in the large bed where Maya found comfort and stability. However, one morning after her mother left for an early errand, Freeman, who had usually been standoffish to Maya and Bailey, made Maya touch his genitals. He threatened to kill her brother, Bailey, if Maya told anyone that he made her touch him.[23] Not fully understanding what Freeman had done to her, Maya felt sorry for him and wanted to be close to him. She kept the secret, not knowing then how a secret can sometimes grow and overwhelm the person who keeps it.

For months after this encounter, Freeman ignored Maya, but one morning he raped her. "If you scream," he warned her, "I'm gonna kill you. And if you tell, I'm gonna kill Bailey."[24] Maya was frightened. She felt sick, and she was in such pain that she thought she was dying. She did not know how to tell Mother or Bailey what had really happened. Her mother, who did not suspect the abuse, thought Maya might be getting the measles. Maya thought, "What he [Freeman] did to me, and what I allowed, must have been very bad if already God let me hurt so much."[25]

Emotional and physical pain wracked Maya. The next day, when the bedsheets were changed, Bailey and Mother found the soiled panties Maya had hidden.

Maya was taken to the hospital. Bailey begged Maya to tell him who had committed the rape. Finally, Maya confessed the truth to her nine-year-old brother, and Bailey cried at Maya's bedside.

Mr. Freeman was arrested. Maya had to appear in court. After a series of questions, the attorney asked Maya, "Did the accused touch you before the occasion on which you claimed he raped you?"

Out of fear Maya lied, "No." Years later in her critically acclaimed autobiography *I Know Why the Caged Bird Sings* Maya explained some of her turmoil:

> I couldn't say yes and tell them how he had loved me once for a few minutes. . . . My uncles would kill me and Grandmother Baxter would stop speaking, as she often did when she was angry. And all those people in the courtroom would stone me as they had stoned the harlot in the Bible. And Mother, who thought I was such a good girl, would be so disappointed. But most important, there was Bailey. I had kept a big secret from him.[26]

The court sentenced Freeman to one year and one day, but he was released that very afternoon. The next day Freeman was found kicked to death.

Years later, Maya stated that her seven-and-a-half-year-old logic told her that her own voice had killed Freeman, and it frightened her to realize that her voice had the power to kill people:[27]

> A man was dead because I lied. . . . I could feel the evilness flowing through my body and waiting, pent up, to rush off my tongue if I tried to open my mouth.

I clamped my teeth shut, I'd hold it in. If it escaped, wouldn't it flood the world and all the innocent people?[28]

Maya reasoned that the only thing she could do was to stop talking to people other than Bailey:

> Instinctively, or somehow, I knew that because I loved him so much I'd never hurt him, but if I talked to anyone else that person might die too. Just my breath, carrying my words out, might poison people.[29]

Once again Maya and Bailey moved into their Grandma Baxter's house. For a while Maya's silence was accepted as a result of the tragedy, but eventually the adults lost patience with her. They believed she was being stubborn and bold. They felt offended that she would not speak to them and often punished her for it.[30]

Soon, Maya and Bailey were on another train going back to Stamps, Arkansas. Maya, in her pain, comforted Bailey, who cried his heart out over being separated from his Mother Dear, whom he had grown to love so much.

3

HEALING WORDS

aya retreated into the cocoon of Stamps, Arkansas. She withdrew into silence, speaking only when necessary. Words written and spoken by others often became a comfort during this difficult time. The words William Shakespeare had written in sixteenth-century England spoke to Maya Angelou in twentieth-century Stamps, Arkansas:

> *When, in disgrace with fortune and men's eyes,*
> *I alone beweep my outcast state,*
> *And trouble deaf heaven with my bootless cries,*
> *And look upon myself, and curse my fate,*
> *Wishing me like to one more rich in hope,*

Featured like him, like him with friends possess'd,
Desiring this man's art and that man's scope.[1]

Maya remembered her reaction when she first heard these meaningful words. "I wept because I thought myself certainly in disgrace with fortune being black and poor and female in the South. And I was also out of grace with men's eyes because I wasn't pretty."[2]

Mrs. Bertha Flowers, a beautiful African-American woman in Stamps who wore printed dresses and flowered hats, reached out to Maya. Flowers, aware of Maya's self-imposed silence, invited the nine-year-old to her home and served her iced lemonade and buttery vanilla tea cookies she had made especially for the child. Flowers told Maya, "Poetry was music written for the human voice."[3] In her soft voice, she began reading Charles Dickens's *A Tale of Two Cities* to Maya: "It was the best of times and the worst of times." Maya heard the music.

Flowers insisted, "Take this book of poems and memorize one for me. Next time you pay me a visit, I want you to recite."[4] How could Maya refuse this gentle lady? Maya scooched under her grandmother's high bed and recited the poems she had heard in her head. Now the carefully chosen words rolling off her tongue sounded so beautiful. They brought comfort to Maya's troubled world. Maya credited Flowers. "It was through her and poetry that I began to talk."[5]

During a visit to the library, Flowers instructed Maya to read the books beginning with A and to continue all the way to Z. Maya read all the books in the school library, not always understanding every word, but reading for the joy of it. "Those books showed me doors which led to degrees of freedom," Maya said.[6] Maya remembered Bertha Flowers as "the measure of what a human being can be. . . . It would be safe to say that she made me proud to be a Negro [African American], just by being herself."[7]

Sometimes Maya pretended to be a character from the books. Sometimes she imagined herself the author. She often reread books she liked, such as Charlotte Brontë's *Jane Eyre*. Maya recalled in an 1983 interview:

> Why would I, a black girl in the South, fall in love with Tolstoy or Dickens? I was Danton and Madame Defarge and all those people in *A Tale of Two Cities*. I was Daphne du Maurier and the Brontë sisters in a town where blacks were not allowed to cross the street. I was educated by these writers. Not about themselves and their people, but about me, what I could hope for.[8]

Maya heard these writers telling her that:

> There was something in her that could be molded, shaped, developed, something of beauty that would make people forget or look beyond the physical. . . . Those writers—some physically dead, some physically alive, all spiritually alive in her—made Maya Angelou pretty.[9]

At the age of nine Maya began writing. Some of her early attempts are contained in a school journal now stored in the Rare Books Division at Wake Forest University. The young Maya described a family traveling to Arkansas:

> Such jolting, rumbling, squeaking, and creaking! Such ringing of cowbells as the cattle plodded along! . . . You were going to settle on some of the rich land in Arkansas. And you were going there not on a train of railroad cars—there weren't any—but in a train of covered wagons, pulled by strong oxen.[10]

As a young girl in Stamps, Maya began to tune into everything around her, "And for a long time I would think of myself, of my whole body, as an ear, and that I could just go into a room and I could absorb sound."[11] In *I Know Why the Caged Bird Sings* Maya recounts a scene at Momma's Store, where on a June night many African Americans gathered around a radio listening to the fight where Joe Louis, a well-respected African-American prizefighter, opposed Italian boxer Primo Carnera. After some tense moments, Maya and the other listeners heard the words they longed to hear: "The winnah, and still heavyweight champeen of the world . . . Joe Louis." His success seemed to ease the sting of the messages blacks received from some whites, "accusations that we were lower types of human beings."[12]

One day, when ten-year-old Maya wandered away from a summer picnic fish fry, she met her first friend, Louise Kendricks. The two girls enjoyed playing croquet, jacks, and hopscotch, going on blackberry hunts, and "falling in the sky," a pretend game. Maya never talked to Louise about the rape in St. Louis, but they shared other secrets of growing up. One February Maya received a note from a schoolmate named Tommy Valdon. "Times are hard and friends are few. I take great pleasure in writing you. Will you be my Valentine?" Maya found comfort in revealing her feelings to Louise.

Maya did well at school, and at age twelve she looked forward to her eighth grade graduation. She had perfect attendance and was one of the top students in her class. "I had outdistanced unpleasant sensations

Arkansas cotton growers at a country store in the late 1930s.

by miles. . . . Years of withdrawal were brushed aside and left behind, as hanging ropes of parasitic moss."[13] Graduation morning was like Christmas morning, and Maya thanked God for allowing her to live to see this day. The graduation present from her grandmother and Uncle Willie, a special-order Mickey Mouse watch, delighted her. The nickels and dimes from the Store customers, accompanied by such encouraging words as "Keep on moving to higher ground" made her feel important.[14] Bailey presented her with a beautiful soft leather-bound copy of poems by Edgar Allan Poe, and that day they walked barefoot in the garden reciting "Annabel Lee":[15]

And neither the angels in Heaven above
Nor the demons down under the sea,
Can ever dissever my soul from the soul
Of the beautiful Annabel Lee.[16]

Feeling special in her butter-yellow piqué graduation dress, Maya anticipated the ceremonies. The day's happiness was taken from her, however, by the white graduation speaker, Edward Donleavy, an education official who had traveled from Texarkana to speak to the graduates. He told them about the plans for new microscopes, chemistry equipment, and art programs—for the white school—and the promise of a paved playing field for sports and some new home economics and shop equipment for their school. He praised two former graduates—one for being a good football tackler, and the other for being a great basketball player.

Maya recounted:

> The man's dead words fell like bricks around the auditorium and too many settled in my belly. . . . The white kids were going to have a chance to become Galileos and Madame Curies and Edisons and Gauguins, and our boys (the girls weren't even in on it) would try to be Jesse Owenses or Joe Louises.[17]

Jesse Owens and Joe Louis were African-American heroes, but Maya took offense at the speaker's implication that the graduates' only heroes, their only role models, could excel only in sports. She resented Donleavy's assumption that her classmates would become maids and farmers, handymen, and washerwomen and should not dream of other careers.[18]

His message made all Maya's accomplishments seem like nothing. "It was awful to be Negro and have no control over my life. It was brutal to be young and already trained to sit quietly and listen to charges brought against my color with no chance of defense."[19]

Then Henry Reed, valedictorian of Maya's class, read his prepared speech. His hope and enthusiasm were not destroyed by the speaker's demoralizing announcements. He turned to his class and led them in singing "Lift Ev'ry Voice and Sing," which was known as the Negro National Anthem. Its well-known and well-loved lyrics were written by one of Maya's favorite poets, James Weldon Johnson, and for generations the song had been sung in African-American churches and schools and at meetings of African-American organizations:[20]

Lift ev'ry voice and sing
Till earth and heaven ring
Ring with the harmonies of Liberty.

She had sung the words many times, but this was the first time she felt a connection with them.[21]

We have come over a way that with tears
has been watered.
We have come, treading our path through
the blood of the slaughtered.

Maya's faith was restored. "I was no longer simply a member of the proud graduating class of 1940; I was a proud member of the wonderful, beautiful Negro race."[22]

Soon after graduation, the sweetness of too many candy bars from the Store's candy counter caused Maya two cavities so painful that neither crushed aspirins nor oil of cloves helped. Her teeth were so rotted to the gums that even Momma's technique of pulling them out with string would not work. The closest black dentist was twenty-five miles away, but Momma remembered that during the hard times of the Great Depression she had lent money to Stamps's white dentist, Dr. Lincoln. Even though few white dentists treated black patients, Momma was sure Dr. Lincoln would return a favor now and help Maya.

Maya and Momma waited in the harsh sunlight near the back entrance to his office for over an hour, only to hear Dr. Lincoln tactfully explain to them that he could not treat African Americans. When Momma persisted, he became angry, and his cruel words stung Maya. "Now, my policy is I'd rather stick my hand in a dog's mouth than in a nigger's."[23] Momma insisted Maya wait outside while she went inside to talk to him again. Although Momma and Maya had to travel twenty-five miles in the back of a Greyhound bus to the nearest African-American dentist in Texarkana, Maya later learned her courageous grandmother had managed to get $10 from the white dentist to help pay for their bus fare.

Not long after this incident Bailey, too, sampled firsthand the hatred many whites had for blacks. He had seen the dead body of an African-American man pulled from the river, and in horror he discovered that the man's genitals had been cut off. "The shock caused him to ask questions that were dangerous for a black boy in 1940 Arkansas."[24] Bailey's questions sought explanations for inequality and hate. Grandmother Henderson decided her grandchildren would be much better off in California, a state "where lynchings were unheard of and a bright young Negro boy could go places. And even his sister might find a niche for herself."[25] Daddy Bailey and Mother Dear were both living in California; one of them would provide a home for Maya and Bailey.

So the Johnson children left Stamps—first Maya, and a month later, when finances permitted, Bailey. Maya carried with her the scars of bigotry, but she also carried the love and strength of people who had reached out to her. She had enjoyed minding the Store, learning Bible verses and church songs, and being loved and protected by Momma and Uncle Willie. She had grown from the kindness of Bertha Flowers and Louise Kendricks.

Writer Lawrence Toppman explained that Maya's experience in Stamps "left her with a fierce dignity and the rugged beauty of a cliff that has been battered by the wind but refuses to crumble."[26] These qualities helped her face the challenges that lay ahead.

4

CALIFORNIA

aya, Bailey, and Mother Dear traveled in Mother's big car to the San Francisco, California, area. The children missed their grandmother, who had returned to Stamps to be with Uncle Willie, but they were charmed with their mother's songs, stories, and explanations of important places along the highway. "Nothing could have been more magical than to have found her at last, and have her solely to ourselves in the closed world of a moving car," Maya recalled.[1]

And the magic continued. During the middle of one ordinary night, Mother Dear, who sometimes called Maya "Ritie" (short for Marguerite) or "Baby," wakened her children just to entertain them with her laughter, dancing, singing, homemade biscuits, and hot cocoa. Mother Dear introduced them to Chinese restaurants and Italian pizza parlors and instructed them to use good table manners and to tip waiters and waitresses properly. She made sure Maya and Bailey tasted Hungarian goulash and Irish stew. Maya remembered, "Through food we learned that there were other people in the world."[2]

Thirteen-year-old Maya loved the beauty, excitement, and freedom of living in a city. She later recalled:

> In San Francisco, for the first time, I perceived myself as part of something. . . . The city became for me the ideal of what I wanted to be as a grown-up. Friendly but never gushing, cool but not frigid or distant, distinguished without the awful stiffness.[3]

In December 1941, as Maya and Bailey adjusted to their new life in California, the United States adjusted to its involvement in World War II. San Francisco played a great role during this war, by becoming the world's largest shipbuilding center and the site of the largest base of the United States Navy. Thousands of service people were stationed in or near the city.

Even though Maya loved San Francisco, she was aware that racism existed in this city, too. After the bombing of Pearl Harbor, West Coast Japanese-Americans, two-thirds of whom were American citizens, were subjected to much hatred. Many were uprooted from their homes and taken to detention camps. Very few non-Japanese protested this grave injustice. Maya remembered, "The Asian population dwindled before my eyes."[4] The arrival in San Francisco of southern blacks and whites who had come to work in the war plants brought its own set of problems, too. Maya explained:

> Southern white illiterates brought their biases . . . from the hills of Arkansas and the swamps of Georgia. The Black ex-farmers had not left their distrust and fear of whites. . . . These two groups were obliged to work side by side in the war plants, and their animosities festered and opened like boils on the face of the city.[5]

During Maya's first semester at San Francisco's George Washington High School, she was one of three African-American students in the entire school. Maya feared being away from people of her race and was disappointed that she "was not the most brilliant or even nearly the most brilliant student."[6] The white students seemed to have better vocabularies than she did and were less afraid of responding in class. Maya, not wishing to draw any negative attention to herself, raised her hand only when she was sure of her answer.

Miss Marie Kirwin, her civics and current events teacher, built up Maya's self-esteem. Kirwin treated all her students with respect: No special treatment was offered to students who gave excellent answers, nor were grudges held against students who misbehaved or gave incorrect answers. Maya was impressed that Kirwin rarely used the textbook and admired that she encouraged them to read newspapers and magazines and discuss the articles they read.[7] Years later Maya would make several visits to this special teacher.

In addition to her high school studies, Maya won a scholarship to the California Labor School, where she took evening drama and dance classes with both black

George Washington High School in San Francisco, California, had an enrollment of approximately two thousand students.

🔲🔲🔲🔲🔲🔲🔲🔲🔲🔲🔲🔲🔲🔲🔲🔲🔲🔲🔲🔲🔲🔲🔲🔲🔲🔲🔲🔲🔲🔲🔲

and white adults. As Maya watched one of her dance teachers move gracefully across the floor, she told herself that she, too, would learn to dance like that. Bailey and Mother encouraged her. "In my mother's house I had often been called to show what I was studying at dance school. The overstuffed chairs were pulled back and I would dance in the cleared living-room space."[8] Years later Maya would study dance with Pearl Primus in New York City and would teach dance in Rome and Tel Aviv.

When she was not busy with classes, Maya went home to her family's fourteen-room house, which was filled with a variety of boarders. Her mother had a new husband, Daddy Clidell Jackson, a hardworking, kind, and humble man who won Maya's admiration. Daddy Clidell taught Maya poker and blackjack, card games that entertained Maya and sharpened her mathematics skills.

Maya's early days in California were relatively happy ones, and when she received an invitation from her father to spend a summer with him in southern California, she thought her happiness would increase. Events would prove her wrong.

Maya, then fifteen years old and nearly six feet tall, was a disappointment to her father's girlfriend, Dolores Stockland, who, for some unknown reason, had been told by Maya's father that his daughter was eight years old. Maya soon came to the conclusion that Stockland

Miss Marie Kirwin, from George Washington High School's history department, was Maya's favorite teacher.

was "mean and petty and full of pretense" and felt that Stockland did not like her because Maya was "tall and arrogant and wasn't clean enough for her."[9] They tried to get along, but the situation became explosive after Daddy Bailey took Maya on a little trip to Mexico without Stockland.

In Mexico, Daddy Bailey became so drunk that he passed out in the back of their car. Maya did not want to spend the night in the car, and Daddy Bailey was in no condition to drive. Maya did not know how to drive, but she was determined to get them home. After strangers helped start the car and point it in the right direction, Maya steered the car down a mountainside. She navigated successfully for nearly fifty miles, before she crashed into the side of another car at a border checkpoint. No one was hurt, but one or two children who had been in the other car involved in the crash had to jump up and down on her father's chest to wake him. Daddy Bailey took over but said very little to Maya the rest of the way home.

More trouble lay ahead. At home Daddy Bailey and Dolores Stockland argued, and Daddy Bailey stormed out. Maya tried to console Stockland, who verbally attacked Maya's mother. An offended Maya slapped Stockland and a fight erupted. Stockland got an octopus hold on Maya's waist that could not be broken until Maya shoved her onto the sofa. Maya fled and sought refuge in her father's car. Stockland followed with a hammer in her hand, circling the car "screaming like a banshee, her face bedizened with fury."[10]

Neighbors finally calmed Stockland down. Daddy Bailey came to the car and soon realized that Maya's side was bleeding. Fearing a scandal if word spread that Bailey Johnson's lady friend had injured his daughter, Daddy Bailey avoided the hospital emergency room and instead took Maya to a friend's house for treatment. Since the cut was not too deep, Daddy Bailey's friend cleansed the wound with witch hazel and dressed it with extra-long Band-Aids™.

Remembering the tension of the night and Stockland's warning that Bailey better not bring her back into the house, Maya stayed with her father's friends. When she realized that she could not go back to her father, and feared that more violence might occur if her mother learned what Stockland had done, she ran away.

Maya wandered the southern California streets pondering her future. She stopped at penny arcades and read science fiction at the library. Eventually she discovered a junkyard filled with old cars, which became her home for one month. Amid the discarded Fords and De Sotos, she met other homeless teenagers of different races, and together they worked at odd jobs and pooled their money. Once Maya and a friend contributed ten dollars by winning second prize in a dance contest. As Maya's new friends accepted her, she began to feel more secure. Maya later said this four-week experience "set a tone of tolerance for my life."[11]

After a month, Maya phoned her mother and asked to come home. When she returned to San Francisco, Maya longed to share her adventures with Bailey, who had always been a good listener, but Bailey seemed more interested in spending time with those "slick street boys" who became his friends rather than listening to Maya's summer adventures.

Bailey loved his Mother Dear and began to show it by imitating the grown-up men who were her friends. Mother Dear loved Bailey, but he was only sixteen, and she would not tolerate his attempt at adult behavior. After weeks of arguments, Bailey decided to live on his own. His departure upset Maya. Now her room "had all the cheeriness of a dungeon and the appeal of a tomb."[12] Maya needed a change to get her through this disappointment. She decided to take time off from school and get a job. Mother Dear approved, since Maya was already a year ahead in school.

After considering several options and realizing that some jobs required a birth certificate verifying her age, Maya longed to be a conductor on a noisy San Francisco trolley, calling out to passengers in her rich voice, "Step forward in the car, please." She wanted to wear the official blue serge suit and a money changer around her waist. Her goal was difficult to achieve: African Americans were not permitted to work on the trolleys. As would be true many times in her life, however, obstacles only made Maya more determined. Her mother offered her encouragement: "Give it everything you've got. I've told you many times, 'Can't do is like Don't Care.' Neither of them have a home."[13]

At the Market Street Railway Company, a receptionist informed Maya that only applicants from employment agencies were being considered. Maya reminded her that the job had been listed in the morning paper. She asked to speak to the personnel manager, but the receptionist said the personnel manager would not be in until tomorrow. When Maya asked the manager's name, the receptionist answered reluctantly but cautioned Maya that he might not be in tomorrow either. Others might have given up after this frustrating encounter, but Maya told herself she would succeed.[14]

For three weeks Maya returned to the musty streetcar office—waiting and hoping. Her mother's faith in her continued to strengthen:

> During this period of strain Mother and I began our first steps on the long path toward mutual adult admiration. She never asked for reports and I didn't offer any details. But every morning she made breakfast, gave me carfare and lunch money, as if I were going to work. She comprehended the perversity of life, that in the struggle lies the joy. That I was no glory seeker was obvious to her, and that I had to exhaust every possibility before giving in was also clear.[15]

Maya's dedication paid off. One day she was asked to fill out an application form. On the form, Maya told "near truths and total lies."[16] She claimed to be nineteen and a former companion and driver for Mrs. Annie Henderson, a white woman in Stamps, Arkansas.

Her strategy worked. At fifteen, she became the first African-American woman conductor on a San Francisco trolley, never dreaming that almost fifty years later she would be the first African-American woman to deliver a poem at a presidential inauguration. Her mother once again showed her support, taking Maya to work as early as 4:30 A.M. or picking her up just before dawn when she got off a split shift.

Maya felt proud and independent.[17] She established a bank account and bought her own clothes. But when

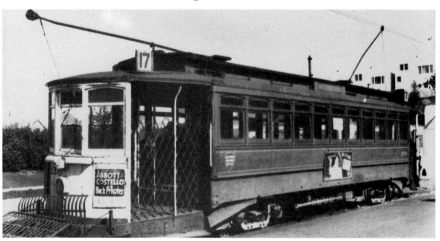

At age fifteen, Maya became the first African-American conductorette on a San Francisco streetcar like this one.

she returned to school after her adventurous summer and her first job, she felt miles apart from her class-mates. They were concerned with football games, winning class offices, and having braces removed, while Maya had experienced "sleeping for a month in a wrecked automobile and conducting a streetcar in the uneven hours of the morning."[18]

Bailey had often told Maya she was pretty, but Maya never agreed. At sixteen she became even more concerned with her appearance. Her hands and feet seemed so much larger than everyone else's, her voice much deeper than those of other girls her age, and she mourned that her breasts were underdeveloped. She worried about her sexuality, too.[19] After reading about lesbians, she wondered if she, too, would be sexually attracted to other women. Later, in her auto-biography, she would explain:

> I wanted to be a woman, but that seemed to me to be a world to which I was to be eternally refused entrance. . . . What I needed was a boyfriend. A boyfriend would clarify my position to the world and, even more important, to myself. A boyfriend's acceptance of me would guide me into that strange and exotic land of frills and femininity. . . . I was being crushed by two unrelenting forces: the uneasy suspicion that I might not be a normal female and my newly awakening sexual appetite.[20]

To quiet some of her confusion, Maya decided to have sex with a good-looking, popular, and conceited boy in her neighborhood. She approached him. He agreed. There was no tenderness or romance in the encounter. Three weeks later, "having thought very little of the strange and strangely empty night," Maya discovered she was pregnant.[21]

Maya forced herself to accept responsibility for her actions and their consequences. "I had to face the fact that I had brought my new catastrophe upon myself. . . . I hefted the burden of pregnancy at sixteen onto my shoulders where it belonged. Admittedly, I staggered under the weight."[22]

Maya turned to her strength, her brother Bailey, who was at sea with the merchant marines. He advised Maya not to tell Mother, for he feared she would make Maya quit school. Bailey encouraged Maya to stay in school, and he cautioned her that once she left it would be difficult to return. Maya took Bailey's advice and kept the pregnancy from her mother, who, unaware that her daughter was pregnant, went on a trip to Alaska as Maya's sixth month of pregnancy approached.

Two days after V-J Day, in August 1945, seventeen-year-old Maya received her high school diploma. On graduation night she informed her parents of her pregnancy by leaving a note.

Dear Parents,

I am sorry to bring this disgrace on the family, but I am pregnant.

Marguerite[23]

Maya had carried the baby eight months and one week without her mother and Daddy Clidell knowing. When they learned the news, they stood by Maya, making sure she saw a doctor and had maternity dresses for herself and clothes for the baby.

The healthy baby boy was named Clyde Bailey Johnson. Mother Dear helped her daughter adjust to the new responsibilities of motherhood. Maya later praised her mother's attitude toward life: "She was Vivian Baxter Jackson. Hoping for the best, prepared for the worst, and unsurprised by anything in between."[24]

At first Maya was afraid to touch her baby son. She dreaded changing his diapers, and she feared dropping him. After three weeks, her wise mother took Clyde to sleep with Maya, who at first was terrified she would roll over and crush her newborn son.[25] Soon Maya began to bond with this innocent creature, and they faced their uncertain future together.

5

"AWAY FROM THE EDGE"

aya desperately wanted to go to college, so Mother and Daddy Clidell offered to have Clyde live with them, but she refused. Arrogance, insecurity, and guilt over being unmarried and unemployed plagued her.[1] Maya also remembered how her own mother had left her with others until she was thirteen. "I took my son and we left home, and I had no understanding about anything—I mean, utterly, so stupid that my face burns to think of it now. But I had the determination to raise my child."[2] Maya's formal education stopped, but her lessons in life continued.

At seventeen she became a busgirl and then a creole cook. "The Creole Café steamed with onion vapor, garlic mists, tomato fogs and green-pepper sprays. I cooked and sweated among the cloying odors and loved being there."[3] Maya rented a room in a San Francisco Victorian house, bought her first furniture, and hired an elderly white woman to be Clyde's babysitter.

At the restaurant she met Curly, a handsome thirty-one-year-old Navy man with dark-brown skin, deep black eyes, and a strong and gentle disposition. He was honest with her and told her that he and his girlfriend would soon get married. Maya ignored this information. She admired the affection Curly showed to her baby and treasured the times when they took Clyde to the park or rode on the Ferris wheel at the beach. Maya longed to marry Curly, but he left, as he had said he would. She endured the painful loss of a first love. She remembered in her second book *Gather Together in My Name*, "Because he had not lied, I was forbidden anger. Because he had patiently and tenderly taught me love, I could not use hate to ease the pain. I had to bear it."[4]

Depression set in, and she began to lose more weight from her thin frame. "By eighteen I managed to look run down if not actually run over,"[5] she wrote. Maya shared her sorrow with Bailey. Again he proved to be her "savior,"[6] just as he had when they were younger. Bailey advised his sister to stop feeling sorry for herself and to get on with her life.

Following Bailey's advice, Maya moved to San Diego. She worked as a cocktail waitress, and customers rewarded her speedy and friendly service with good tips. Baby Clyde was left in the loving care of Henry and Cleo Jenkins, child-care providers, whose home and manner reminded Maya of her own beloved grandmother in Stamps, Arkansas.

Maya took dance classes, dressed in off-the-shoulder embroidered blouses and long, boldly flowered skirts, and fantasized about a better life for Clyde and herself. She continued to read, discovering the Russian writers Dostoevsky, Gorki, Chekhov, and Turgenev. She explained her passion: "The books couldn't last long enough for me. I wished the writers all alive, turning out manuscripts for my addiction."[7]

During her late teens, Maya continued to work as a waitress, but cooked up a scheme she would regret: She rented a house in her name, paid all the bills, set two prostitutes up in business, and took a percentage of what they made. Although Maya was not a prostitute, she soon realized what tragedy could befall her. "I was sitting in the back of the taxi when a numbing thought sidled across my brain like a poisonous snake. I might be declared an unfit mother and my son would be made a ward of the court."[8] In a panic, Maya took her baby and returned to Stamps, Arkansas.

There Uncle Willie and Momma welcomed Maya and Clyde. Pleasant memories of early days in Stamps flooded back, but the hurtful times surfaced, too, for the town was still divided by "railroad tracks, the swift Red River, and racial prejudice,"[9] as Maya would realize once more.

One summer morning, Maya took a three-mile walk into the white part of Stamps to pick up a Simplicity sewing pattern she had ordered from the General Merchandise Store. In an aisle too narrow for two people to walk freely, Maya met a tall salesperson. After a few awkward attempts, the white salesperson ordered Maya to stand still so she could pass. Maya bristled. Angered that the salesperson had treated her as a servant, Maya commanded, "No, you stand still and I'll pass around you."[10] The verbal confrontation continued. Insults were exchanged. Maya left without her pattern, feeling proud she had taken a stand.[11]

Her moment of triumph did not last long. Momma, who had already received a phone call reporting the incident, waited for Maya on the porch. Maya tried to defend her behavior at the store by stating that it was a matter of principle. Momma slapped Maya across the face, something Momma had never done before. Maya cried and protested, but the slaps continued until Maya found herself lying in the soft dust in front of the porch. She remembered, "I didn't want to move. I never wanted to get up again."[12]

Momma demanded that Maya stand up. As she rose and looked into Momma's wide face, Maya heard Momma's explanation for her anger:

> You think 'cause you've been to California these crazy people won't kill you? You think them lunatic cracker boys won't try to catch you in the road and violate you? You think because of your all-fired principle some of the men won't feel like putting their white sheets on and riding over here to stir up trouble? You do, you're wrong. Ain't nothing to protect you and us except the good Lord and some miles. I packed you and the baby's things, and Brother Wilson is coming to drive you to Louisville.[13]

Later, Maya realized that Momma was trying to protect her.[14] That very afternoon Maya and her baby left Stamps in a horse-drawn wagon. More than twenty years would pass before Maya would return to Stamps.

Upon returning to San Francisco and her mother, Maya got a job as a short-order cook in a greasy spoon restaurant. She paid her mother room and board and spent the rest of her money on blues and jazz records and books.

At nineteen Maya tried to provide security for Clyde, but she needed a real profession, and she looked to the Army. The benefits were great, she could learn a trade, and when her enrollment ended, the G.I. Bill would allow her to go back to school and buy a home. Her mother cautioned Maya that the structure of the Army might be hard to deal with, but as usual offered her encouragement. "Government is going to give you an education and a start in life and you're going to give class to that uniform."[15]

Maya realized that if her Army dream were to come true, she would have to lie on the questionnaires and applications when asked if she had children. No one discovered her deceit. Based on her tests and applications, she was accepted into Officer Candidate School. She quit her job so she could spend more time with her baby son before she left for training at Fort Lee, Virginia. Maya hated to leave Clyde, but she knew the training the Army offered promised a better life for them both.[16]

A week before her induction into the United States Army, Maya was accused of lying when she had answered "No" to the question "Have you ever been a member of the Communist Party?" She was shocked, since she had told the truth with that answer.[17] The official reminded her that the California Labor School, which Maya had attended for two years, had been branded a Communist organization. The Army did not bring charges of falsification against Maya, but dismissed her as a security risk. Now, she had no job, she had given her clothes to the Salvation Army, and her books were packed in boxes. Her opportunity was gone.

Dejected, Maya found another job waitressing. Soon a ray of hope entered in the form of R. L. Poole, a dancer from Chicago who invited Maya to become his dance partner after she was recommended to him by a record shop owner. Maya committed herself to dancing and practiced for hours to Charlie Parker's "Cool Breeze." The dance team was known as Poole and Rita. At first Maya experienced stage fright, but then she began to love performing. Bailey Johnson and his new wife, Eunice, encouraged Maya's show business plans, and once again her future looked promising. Then Poole's old girlfriend and dance partner came back into town, and Maya's hopes were dashed. "My career was over before it began," she said later:

> My tears came hot and angry. I had dared so many things and failed. . . . All the doors had slammed shut, and I was locked into a too-tall body, with an unpretty face, and a mind that bounced around like a Ping-Pong ball. I gave in to sadness because I had no choice.[18]

In a manner that was to become characteristic of Maya's approach to life and the defeats it often handed out, Maya did not despair too long:

> I decided I'd try to sort out my life. I tried to crush the thoughts of self-pity that needled into my brain. . . . I had to find a job, get my grits together and take care of my son. So much for show biz, I was off to live real life.[19]

She journeyed eighty miles to Stockton, California, to work as a fry cook in a restaurant owned by her mother's friend. Maya made $60 a week frying hamburgers, pork chops, eggs, and ham steaks. Because of Maya's working hours, Clyde lived with a woman named Big Mary, who was the neighborhood's surrogate mother, and Maya picked him up on her day off.

At the restaurant, nineteen-year-old Maya met the next love of her life, L. D. Tolbrook, a forty-five-year-old gambler who charmed Maya with his "Southern manners and city class."[20] He was a smooth talker, and he promised Maya that he would leave his wife and marry her when the time was right. The naive Maya believed that Tolbrook would provide her with "a life of ease and romance."[21] Instead, when he incurred a gambling debt of $5,000, he talked Maya into prostitution to help him pay his debts. Maya justified her behavior by telling herself she was helping the man she loved.

Her brief and unhappy stint with prostitution ended when she received an emergency call to return home.[22] Her mother had been hospitalized, and Bailey's wife, Eunice, had died of double pneumonia and tuberculosis on the first anniversary of their wedding. Maya remembered Bailey's grief: "He closed in upon himself and smiled the new grimace. I lost part of my brother forever."[23]

Despite Bailey's emotional pain, he still looked out for his sister. He warned her that it was just a matter of time before her darling L. D. Tolbrook, who had led her to prostitution, would make her use cocaine.

Bailey ordered her to get her baby, break off the relationship, and return home.

Maya went to Big Mary's to pick up her son, but Big Mary and Clyde were not there. They were not anywhere. Maya panicked when she realized that Big Mary had disappeared with three-year-old Clyde. She rushed to L. D. Tolbrook's house for help, but he was furious at her, saying that he would help her when he found the time. His mean reaction and unwillingness to help her find her son made it clear that he had used her. "I had been stupid, again. And stupidity had led me into a trap where I had lost my baby."[24] Maya

Maya Angelou admiring a baby picture of her son, Clyde.

had to solve this problem on her own. She had to calm down and find a way to get her baby back. Through her own investigating, she finally found Big Mary in Bakersfield, California. Big Mary asked for forgiveness, explaining that she loved Clyde and meant no harm. She begged Maya to let the baby stay with her awhile. Maya told Big Mary she understood, but she raced out the door with Clyde safely in her arms.

In Oakland, California, Maya became the employee of James Cain, a restaurant owner and promoter of three unknown prizefighters. Cain, whose smile revealed half-carat diamonds in his two front teeth, paid Maya $75 a week to manage his restaurant. Within two months he gave her the job of chauffeur to his three boxers. Dressed in a brown suede outfit, Maya felt on top of the world.[25] She followed the boxers during their morning runs around Lake Merrit and got them to the gym on time, but she lost her job when she overstepped her bounds and embarrassed Cain in front of his friends by demanding that a brutal fight be stopped.

Depression set in once more, and this time Maya stopped believing in herself. "My head stayed high from habit, but my last hope was gone. Every way out of the maze had proved to be a false exit. . . . For the first time in my life I sat down defenseless to await life's next assault."[26]

A week after Cain fired her, one of the restaurant's patrons, a kind, generous African-American man named Troubadour Martin, came to see Maya. He told her he had a connection for ladies' dresses and suits, and he wanted the ladies to come to Maya's home to try on the clothes. The job was ideal. Maya would not have to sell anything, and she would get a percentage of the sales. Maya could spend time with her baby and read. For two months she worked for Troubadour and enjoyed his friendship, although she

Although they were separated for most of Maya's childhood, Maya Angelou and her mother, Vivian Baxter Johnson, developed a close relationship.

suspected that he was addicted to heavy narcotics.[27] Her instincts proved right.

One evening Troubadour took her to see a group of addicts shooting up. He made her watch him shoot heroin into his own veins, then he made her promise she would never get involved in a scene like this. It was a brutal scene to witness, but Maya was forever grateful to Troubadour:

> No one had ever cared for me so much. He had exposed himself to me to teach me a lesson and I learned it as I sat in the dark car inhaling the odors of the wharf. The life of the underworld was truly a rat race, and most of its inhabitants scurried like rodents in the sewers and gutters of the world. I had walked the precipice and seen it all; and at the critical moment, one man's generosity pushed me safely away from the edge.[28]

That night Maya decided to go back to her mother. "I had no idea what I was going to make of my life, but I had given a promise and found my innocence. I swore I'd never lose it again."[29]

6

NEW OPPORTUNITY

During Maya's early twenties, music played an important role in her life. "Music was my refuge," she wrote. "I could crawl into the spaces between the notes and curl my back to loneliness."[1]

Maya collected records and often spent her free time at the Melrose Record Shop in San Francisco, where customers could listen to the selections through earphones before purchasing them. She formed a good relationship with the white owner, Louise Cox. Louise soon hired Maya, who did an effective job ordering records, taking inventory, playing requested records, and dusting off window displays. Maya's days in her grandmother's Store in Stamps had provided excellent training. At work Maya could also listen to the music she loved, from the classical strains of Bartók to the hit parade of new blues tunes:

> And I made my first white friend—the woman who owned the store. She introduced me to another way of life. With her help, I began to give up my ignorance and became aware. I'll never know what she saw in that twenty-year-old, six foot tall, closed, withdrawn black girl. But somehow she was perceptive enough to know she had something to give me.[2]

One of the record store's customers, Tosh Angelos, a Greek sailor, shared Maya's love of music and her devotion to her son, Clyde. When Tosh and Maya married in 1952, Maya quit her job and became a homemaker. As she did with all her other undertakings, she gave 100 percent to her new role. She cooked delicious meals and kept the house spotless. "My floors were dangerous with daily applications of wax and our furniture slick with polish."[3]

Although Maya enjoyed the safety Angelos provided, she soon began to realize that he restricted her freedom. Tosh, an introvert, did not allow many of Maya's and Clyde's friends to visit their home. He told Clyde that there was no God, and Maya had to sneak out of the house to attend church services. Before long, Tosh's gentleness faded and his anger surfaced. Soon he announced he was tired of being married. Maya noted that their house was "weary with failure," and the marriage ended after about two and a half years.[4]

To support herself and Clyde, Maya became a dancer in a club named the Garden of Allah. The customers liked Maya, and her talent attracted the manager of San Francisco's famous basement nightclub The Purple Onion. The club owners wanted her to use a more glamorous and exotic name than Rita Johnson, so they encouraged Maya to use the first name her brother had given her combined with a variation of her ex-husband's last name. From that point on she became known as Maya Angelou.

To prepare for this new role, Angelou had a drama coach who taught her how to stand, walk, and offer her best profile to the audience. Her pianist helped her learn at least twelve songs before opening night. Angelou practiced some of the cute, funny songs in front of Clyde, and he listened attentively. Soon Angelou debuted at The Purple Onion. The voice that had sung gospel songs in the church in Stamps, Arkansas, now delighted the patrons who crowded into the smoke-filled, purple-walled room to hear her sing calypso.

Another career had begun for Maya Angelou. People lined up outside for blocks to see her. Reporters interviewed her. She spoke on the radio, and she sang on television. She even had a ten-member fan club. She remembers:

> I was hired at the club as a singer, but the songs had many refrains and such complex rhythms that often I got lost in the plot and forgot the lyrics. So, when the words eluded me, I would admit my poor memory and add that if the audience would bear with me I would dance.[5]

The audience loved Angelou's honesty as well as her dancing.

Angelou embraced another great opportunity: She got a part in *New Faces of 1953*, a Broadway hit that came out west. Angelou's first big show business break had come, but she was forced to turn down the role because she was still under contract with The Purple Onion. When they would not release her, she despaired, thinking, "I will never have another chance like this again."[6] Realizing she had no other alternative, she reluctantly honored the contract with The Purple Onion.

In her free time, Angelou took voice lessons from Frederick Wilkerson, a teacher she affectionately called Uncle Wilkie. He warned Angelou that if she continued to sing the way she did, she would lose her voice in five years. Angelou heeded his advice and worked very hard to learn proper technique.

Angelou created music for some poems she had written years before, and she composed some new songs that fit the popular calypso form. (Years later she wrote some lyrics for popular singer Roberta

Flack.) Angelou took time off to see George Gershwin's *Porgy and Bess*, and she fell in love with the opera. "I was stunned. *Porgy and Bess* had shown me the greatest array of Negro talent I had ever seen."[7] Angelou longed to be one of the dancers.

Angelou's luck was on the upswing. After she had fulfilled her contract at The Purple Onion, she received an invitation to a New York City audition for Clifford Odets's *House of Flowers*, a new Broadway show in which she would act with the great Pearl Bailey.

A few minutes after Angelou heard she had won the part, she received an offer to play Ruby in the traveling production of *Porgy and Bess*. Two great opportunities arrived at the same time, but she gave up the important role in the new Broadway show for a chorus part in the touring company of *Porgy and Bess* sponsored by the State Department:

> There really was no contest. I wanted to travel, to try to speak other languages, to see the cities I had read about all my life, but most important, I wanted to be with a large, friendly group of Black people who sang so gloriously and lived with such passion.[8]

Once Maya Angelou made the decision to go, the thought of leaving her son tormented her. A friend reminded her that since she was raising Clyde on her own, it was up to Angelou to make a better life for both of them. She reassured Angelou that Clyde would be well taken care of by his grandmother.

Angelou spent a year touring in *Porgy and Bess*. In 1954 and 1955, she traveled in twenty-two countries, including Italy, France, Egypt, and Spain. She remembered one of her first stops in Verona, Italy, the home of William Shakespeare's Romeo Montague and Juliet Capulet, characters whom she had met through her childhood reading:

> I was so excited at the incredible turn of events which had brought me from a past of rejection, of slammed doors and blind alleys, of dead-end streets and cul-de-sacs, into the bright sun of Italy, into a town made famous by one of the world's greatest writers.[9]

Maya Angelou taught herself Italian and longed to speak the language of every country the *Porgy and Bess* company visited. Her preperformance jitters about her debut as Ruby were soon calmed. Their opening night of the European tour was a smash hit. Her fellow cast members gave Angelou congratulatory hugs and kisses and pats on the back. The entire cast received a standing ovation and shouts of "Bravo! Bravo!"

In France, the production was held over for months. In order to be able to send enough money home for Clyde's care, Angelou also worked in Paris, singing in a midnight show at the Mars Club and performing in a second show at the Rose Rouge. Admiring fans sent notes and flowers to her dressing room.

Maya Angelou was a part of a very special group. She and the rest of the *Porgy and Bess* cast were the first American singers to be invited to Communist Eastern Europe and the first to perform American opera at La Scala, the famous opera house in Milan, Italy. The cast traveled to Greece on the famed Orient Express train, and then on to other destinations. Angelou rode camels in Egypt, had her photograph taken in front of the Sphinx, and visited the pyramids.

Porgy and Bess was well received in Athens and in Tel Aviv. In Israel Angelou learned Hebrew folk songs and sang African-American spirituals for the Israelis. She gave classes in modern ballet and African movement in exchange for lessons in Middle Eastern dance. In *Wouldn't Take Nothing for My Journey Now*, Angelou reminds her readers of the value of travel: "Perhaps travel cannot prevent bigotry, but by demonstrating that all peoples cry, laugh, eat, worry, and die, it can introduce the idea that if we try to understand each other, we may even become friends."[10]

Fame and foreign places dazzled Angelou, but letters from Clyde often dimmed the glow. "His letters, printed in large letters, arrived regularly, and each one ended: 'When are you coming home, Mother? Or Can I come to visit you?'" Angelou agonized about being away from him. She missed reading to him and taking him to movies and museums.

Then Angelou received distressing news from home. Clyde had developed a severe rash that did not respond to treatment. Angelou realized she would

🔲🔲🔲🔲🔲🔲🔲🔲🔲🔲🔲🔲🔲🔲🔲🔲🔲🔲🔲🔲🔲🔲🔲🔲🔲🔲🔲🔲🔲🔲🔲🔲🔲🔲🔲🔲🔲

Some members of the *Porgy and Bess* cast sightsee in Athens, Greece. The production opened at the Royal Theater on January 18, 1955.

have to leave the tour. When she announced her resignation, she was informed she would have to pay her own way home as well as the first-class airfare of her replacement. The news shocked her.[11] She would have to earn more than $1,000 before she could go home. Once again she met the challenge and worked three jobs: performing in *Porgy and Bess*, singing in a nightclub, and teaching classes in African movement to some dancers at the Rome Opera House.

When Angelou returned home, she was alarmed by Clyde's skin condition and by his sadness.[12] Clyde clung to her, and she wanted to hold her nine-year-old son every minute. She told him, "I swear to you, I'll never leave you again. If I go, when I go, you'll go with me or I won't go."[13] Nothing seemed to help Clyde's skin condition where his skin flaked with scales. Angelou was tormented by guilt.[14] The tour had given her an outstanding education, but at what cost? "I had ruined my beautiful son by neglect, and neither of us would ever forgive me."[15]

In her despair, the twenty-six-year-old Angelou visited the Langley Porter Psychiatric Clinic, but she could not bring herself to reveal her troubles to the psychiatrist. Instead, she confided in Uncle Wilkie, her friend and voice coach, that she could not see any reason for living since she had done such harm to Clyde. Uncle Wilkie provided the best therapy. He made Angelou write down everything she had to be thankful for, and he made her end her list with the following: "I am blessed. And I am grateful."[16] He told her to get to work, reminded her that she was a good mother, and left her with these words of advice: "Don't ask God to forgive you, for that's already done. Forgive yourself. You're the only person you can forgive. You've done nothing wrong. So forgive yourself."[17]

Gradually, Maya Angelou began to feel better about herself. Clyde's skin healed, and they celebrated by riding bikes and picnicking in Golden Gate Park. Clyde, now relaxed and more independent, announced that he had changed his name to Guy. When Angelou reminded him of Clyde River in Scotland, he replied, "It's an O.K. name for a river, but my name is Guy." Angelou and the rest of the family honored his request.

Good news arrived soon. Angelou received a contract to perform at The Clouds in beautiful Hawaii. At Angelou's insistence, transportation and accommodations were also provided for Guy. She delighted in seeing her name on the hotel marquee of The Clouds, but she was more delighted that she was Guy's mother and that he was her "wonderful, dependently independent son."[18]

7

STRIVING TO
BE FREE

s the 1950s ended and the new decade began, Maya Angelou dared to take more risks and encountered fascinating experiences in the city of New York and the continent of Africa.

As the country was about to embark on a new era of social change, Angelou embarked on a new career in writing. "At first I limited myself to short sketches, then to song lyrics, then I dared stories."[1]

In the late 1950s, John Oliver Killens, a prominent figure in the African-American literary community, had been in Hollywood writing a screenplay based on his first novel, *Youngblood*. He agreed to read some of Angelou's works in progress. He felt her writing showed promise, and he invited her to come to New York and join the Harlem Writers Guild, a group of talented African-American writers who met informally to critique each other's writing.

He told Angelou, "Most of your work needs polishing. In fact, most of everybody's work could stand rewriting. But you have undeniable talent." Angelou had written and recorded six songs for Liberty Records, but she did not seriously consider writing as a career until Killens gave her his critique.[2] His encouragement welcomed her into the world of writing, and he and his wife, Grace, helped Angelou and Guy settle in Brooklyn, New York.

As Angelou read her new play, *One Love, One Life*, to the writer's group, fear consumed her:

> The blood pounded in my ears but not enough to drown the skinny sound of my voice. My hands shook so that I had to lay the pages in my lap, but that was not a good solution due to the tricks my knees were playing. They lifted voluntarily, pulling my heels off the floor and then trembled like disturbed Jello.[3]

How wonderful it would have been if praise had filled the room after her reading, but the initial comments were razor sharp. "I found no life and very little love in the play from the opening act to its unfortunate end," one listener remarked.[4] The other reactions were not very positive either. Angelou wanted to bolt from the room and never return to another meeting of the Harlem Writers Guild, but Killens warned her to toughen up or she would miss out on some valuable suggestions that would improve her writing. Angelou stayed, and before the night ended, she received important advice, ". . . Write each sentence over and over again, until it seems you've used every combination possible, then write it again," advised group member John Henrik Clarke, who had been critical of Angelou's play.[5]

". . . Lots of people have more talent than you or I. Hard work makes the difference. Hard, hard unrelenting work,"[6] said Paule Marshall, another group member and author of the highly praised *Brown Girl, Brownstones*.

Angelou's ability to recover quickly from the sting of the criticism and learn from it allowed her to remain part of this talented group. She was determined to be a writer. She became friends with many members, including the author Rosa Guy, whose beautifully crafted novels include *The Friends*, *The Disappearance*, and *My Love, My Love, or the Peasant Girl*.

Writing did not pay the bills, so Angelou used her skill as a performer to earn a living. The New York move brought Angelou to Harlem's famed Apollo Theater. As she graced its legendary stage in her sky-blue chiffon gown and matching heels, she did something the manager warned her not to do; because he felt she would be laughed off the stage. Determined to do things her way, Angelou asked the audience to join in singing an African song called "Uhuru" (Swahili for "freedom") taught to her by the great Nigerian drummer Babatunda Olatunje.

She explained to members of the audience, "If you believe you deserve freedom, if you really want it, if you believe it should be yours, you must sing:

> *U hu uhuru oh yea freedom*
> *U hu uhuru oh yea freedom*
> *Uh huh Uh hum.*[7]

The audience did not laugh Angelou off the stage as the manager had predicted; instead, they sang the refrain passionately as the rhythms of the conga drums, timbales, and caracas filled the theater.

Angelou recalled this proud moment in her book *The Heart of a Woman*:

> Even as I bowed, I knew the applause was only in small part for me. I had been merely the ignition which set off their fire. It was our history, our painful passage and uneven present that burned luminously in the dark theater.[8]

Freedom for all was the dream of many in the early 1960s. Young people across America, black and white, participated in sit-ins and freedom rides in the segregated South as a means of peaceful protest against racial discrimination. People of courage took the lead in trying to make the North aware of their struggle. Angelou met some of these heroic individuals who came North including Ralph Abernathy, Wyatt Tee Walker, Martin Luther King, Jr., and Andrew Young.

Angelou heard Dr. Martin Luther King, Jr.'s, message of hope delivered in a Harlem church. King was in New York raising money for the Southern Christian Leadership Conference (SCLC), an organization founded by King and other civil rights leaders to coordinate civil rights work in the South. His words inspired her and her friend, actor-comedian Godfrey Cambridge. They did more than listen, they sought permission from the SCLC to raise money for the cause. Years later, Angelou remembered King as "a magnificent spirit . . . a great spiritual leader and an extraordinary man."[9]

Angelou thought a play would be a wonderful fund-raiser, but after attempting to write a play on the theme of liberation, she soon became discouraged. Every plot she tried seemed unappealing, and her characters seemed so unreal that they even bored Angelou. Godfrey Cambridge eased her despair by suggesting a different format—an informal revue of actors, singers, dancers, and comedians. Angelou and Cambridge helped to organize the entertainers in the 1960 revue called *Cabaret for Freedom* at the Village Gate, a well-known nightclub of the time. The performers both delighted and inspired the audiences in a successful fund-raiser for the SCLC. As a finale, the entire cast joined to sing the words that Angelou and her classmates had sung at her eighth grade graduation in Stamps, Arkansas—James Weldon Johnson's "Lift Ev'ry Voice and Sing."

Her organizational skills soon earned Angelou the important job of northern coordinator for the Southern Christian Leadership Conference at age thirty-two. During the months that she had this job, Angelou organized student volunteers. She helped send out tens of thousands of letters and invitations signed by King, made hundreds of statements in his name, and contacted philanthropists, seeking their contributions. In *Heart of a Woman*, Angelou wrote:

> Days were crammed with phone calls, taxi rides and serious letters reminding the mailing list that freedom was costly and that a donation of any amount was a direct blow against the citadel of oppression which held a helpless people enthralled.[10]

She continued attending Harlem Writers Guild meetings, honing her craft.

Angelou's dedication inspired her son during his teenage years, and Guy also became involved in causes, protest marches, and politics. He did well in school and worked part-time at a bakery to help out with expenses. Angelou was strict about his curfew, and he honored it. Angelou and Guy still played Scrabble™, a game they had enjoyed together when Guy was a child. Guy went to the movies, the zoo, and

Coney Island with Angelou and her fiancé, Thomas Allen, a divorced bail bondsman.

Allen was kind to Guy and Angelou, but she regretted that he really was not interested in her work at the SCLC or in her beliefs about important issues. She knew she did not love Allen, but she felt lonely and thought she would make a good wife.[11]

Soon she met Vasumzi Make (pronounced Mah-kay), a South African freedom fighter who was interested in issues close to Angelou's heart. She fell instantly in love with Vus, as he was called. Vus Make had escaped from South Africa, and had journeyed to the United States to petition the United Nations to end South Africa's racial policy of apartheid and to support the cry for freedom of Africans who lived under this unjust system. (Until 1991, apartheid was the South African government's policy of rigid racial segregation and official mistreatment of non-whites.)

Angelou respected Make and his great work, and she knew she could help him with his struggle to gain freedom for blacks in South Africa. She admired his kindness and gentleness toward Guy. When Make proposed to Angelou while she was still engaged to Allen, the promise of a life of adventure and the gift of an African father for Guy made Angelou break the engagement with Allen. Angelou and Make soon married.

Make worked hard to help others gain their freedom, but he had a difficult time accepting Angelou's independence. When she had an opportunity to perform as the White Queen in the French playwright Jean Genet's off-Broadway play *The Blacks*, a play that mirrored the "real-life confrontations that were occurring daily in America's streets,"[12] Make refused to let her perform. "No wife of an African leader can go on the stage," he declared.[13]

However, after reading the play, Make gave his approval. Angelou accepted the role. The author James Baldwin, who became Angelou's lifelong friend, often attended rehearsals. Angelou performed with notable African-American performers, including Lou Gossett, Jr.; James Earl Jones; and Cicely Tyson. Angelou cowrote two songs for the production, and she did such an excellent job in the role of the White Queen that even Make was impressed. Angelou said:

> I used the White Queen to ridicule mean white women and brutal white men who had too often injured me and mine. Every inane posture and haughty attitude I had ever seen found its place in my White Queen.[14]

Angelou left the successful play when the producer refused to pay her for the songs she had composed with Ethel Ayler. Angelou subsequently spent most of her time keeping a beautiful apartment for Make, who did not always appreciate her efforts. He did not like her choice of furniture and was fanatical about the

Maya Angelou, James Baldwin, and Baldwin's mother, Berdis, at Baldwin's sixtieth birthday party in 1984. Angelou and Baldwin remained close friends until his death.

cleanliness of the apartment. She wrote, "Sometimes he would pull the sofa away from the wall to see if possibly I had missed a layer of dust."[15] Make paid the bills and gave her a generous food and house allowance, but Angelou missed her independence, and her "heart was not at peace."[16] She suspected Make had been unfaithful to her.[17] She felt lost, and she withdrew from her friends and from the activities of the Harlem Writers Group.

Angelou dreaded answering the telephone after she began receiving anonymous phone calls, probably from South Africa's security police, reporting that harm had been done to Guy or Make. Worry consumed her.[18] But, fortunately, the threats were never carried out. She also faced the embarrassment of being evicted from her apartment when she discovered that Make had not paid the bills. Guy comforted Angelou, "It'll be okay, Mom. We'll live through this one, too." And they did. Angelou, Make, and Guy moved into a musty hotel for several weeks before moving to Cairo, Egypt.

Cairo was a mixture of camels and limousines, skyscrapers and street vendors. Angelou and Guy made a bet about who would develop the largest Arabic vocabulary and speak in the best accent. They were excited about being in this new environment, where Egyptian officials supported the African struggle for freedom.[19]

Make continued both his noble freedom work and his bad habit of not paying his bills. To help out with expenses, Angelou took a job as associate editor of *The Arab Observer*, an English news weekly published in the Middle East. Make was angry when Angelou took the job. His anger at Angelou's independence and her continuing suspicions of his affairs with other women hurt their relationship. Angelou was no longer in love with Make, but she continued to live with him. She admired and respected his work and the devotion he showed to Guy.

Maya Angelou did not have experience as a journalist, but she approached her job as associate editor as she approached every other challenge—with courage and determination. If Angelou did not understand a task, she would try to learn it. She remembered how valuable libraries had been to her since childhood, and she used the office library for research.

"For two weeks I stayed in the room, using each free moment to cull from the shelves information about journalism, writing, Africa, printing, publishing and editing," Angelou wrote in *The Heart of a Woman*, the fourth volume of her autobiography.[20] She relied on Make's knowledge of the tribes, leaders, topography, and political positions in all the African countries to help her write accurate and informative articles about Africa. She also wrote and sometimes narrated commentary for Radio Egypt.

When Guy graduated from high school in Cairo in 1962, he reminded Angelou that he had gone to more than nineteen schools in eleven years. In the past, family members and school personnel had criticized Angelou for uprooting Guy, claiming he needed security and stability. Angelou had responded:

> . . . but I am his security. Wherever we go, we go together. Wherever he is he knows that that six-foot-tall Black woman is not too far away. What I don't furnish in stability, I make up in love.[21]

After Guy's graduation, Make and Angelou parted as friends. The marriage had only lasted a few years, but her experience in Africa had a positive influence on her life.

Angelou and Guy left Cairo to enroll Guy in the University of Ghana, in Accra. Angelou planned to move to Liberia, where she had a job waiting for her at the Department of Information. As they flew over the Sahara Desert to Ghana in Western Africa, and Angelou viewed the area below, she thought of all her ancestors and the pain they had endured. Later she recorded her feelings in *Heart of a Woman*:

> Here, there, along the banks of that river, someone was taken, tied with ropes, shackled with chains, forced to march for weeks carrying the double burden of neck irons and abysmal fear. In that large clump of trees, looking like wood moss from the plane's great height, boys and girls had been hunted like beasts, caught and tethered together. Sacrificial lambs on the altar of greed.[22]

The misery that had begun centuries before on the African land just below their plane returned to tear Angelou's heart that day. These images of a time long past brought up memories of her past. She relived the hateful looks she had received and remembered the opportunities that had been denied to her because of her skin color. Suddenly the tears poured out. Guy wanted to help, but she could not pour out her feelings to him, and he thought she cried because she felt unloved. He tried to reassure her.[23]

Angelou once told an interviewer, "Life offers us tickets to places which we have not knowingly asked for. (Then it makes us pay the fare.)"[24] Her ticket to Ghana would help her turn her unhappiness and pain into strength.

8

A JOURNEY
OUTWARD AND
INWARD

uring the summer of 1962, after two happy
days in Ghana, Guy was severely injured in
an automobile accident: he broke his neck
and fractured an arm and a leg when a truck plowed
into his car. Angelou canceled her plans to go to
Liberia, and during the next four months, she stayed
by her seventeen-year-old son's side.

After his recovery, Guy began his studies at the
University of Ghana, considered to be the best institution
of higher learning in Africa at that time. During their
stay in Ghana, Angelou worked hard at giving Guy
his independence while still letting him know she

cared for him. Although they did not always agree, Guy appreciated Angelou's patience, love, and generosity. He would soon tell her:

> You have finished mothering a child. You did a very good job. Now, I am a man. Your life is your own, and mine belongs to me. I am not rejecting you, I'm just explaining that our relationship has changed.[1]

Although she only had a high school education, Angelou, in her mid-thirties, worked as an assistant administrator at the University of Ghana. "I challenged myself to do whatever job assigned to me with intense commitment and a good cheerfulness."[2] She typed manuscripts for a professor, organized student files, handled theater reservations, sold tickets at the box office in town, and played the title role in Bertolt Brecht's *Mother Courage*. She stated, "At last life was getting itself in joint."[3] The job was good, but the pay was not, so she continued her career as a journalist at the *Ghanaian Times*. She was also a feature editor of the *African Review*. She used part of her pay to help Guy with his college tuition and books.

In Ghana, Angelou felt at home for the first time in her life. Ghana's president, Kwame Nkrumah, had let it be known that African Americans were welcome in Ghana. Angelou and other African Americans who had so often felt unwanted in America saw promise in this country of their ancestors. "We were Black Americans in West Africa, where for the first time in our lives the color of our skin was accepted as correct and normal."[4] She loved the Ghanaian people, whose skin colors reminded her of her "childhood cravings: peanut butter, licorice, chocolate and caramel."[5] Angelou wore African clothes and learned to speak several African languages, including Fanti. "The music of the Fanti language was becoming singable to me, and its vocabulary was moving orderly into my brain."[6] She learned to prepare and enjoy such West African dishes as tomatoey jollof rice; kontumre, a blend of wild mustard greens and native spices; and pineapple fritters with a cream sauce of coconut milk and rum.

African art fills Maya Angelou's home.

Just as Angelou had been active in the civil rights struggle in America, her commitment to civil rights continued in Africa. On August 28, 1963, in Washington, D.C., over a quarter of a million people of all races joined Dr. Martin Luther King, Jr., in the March on Washington. To support the March, Angelou and about one hundred other African Americans living in Ghana staged a march on the American Embassy. During their protest, they heard the sad news that one of their heroes, Dr. W.E.B. DuBois, the renowned African-American intellectual, had died in Accra. They sang in memory of this great man of intelligence and courage, who had advocated that all people of African descent work together to conquer prejudice. She remembered, "We had walked in the dark, through the flickering light of oil sticks, protesting American racism and extolling the indomitability of the human spirit.[7]

Angelou's stay in Ghana provided her with the opportunity to spend time with Malcolm X, another civil rights leader from the United States. Initially Malcolm X had preached that African Americans should live and work apart from whites and that violence was acceptable in the fight for civil rights, but after his experience in Mecca, where he had made an Islamic pilgrimage in late 1963, his views began to change. He saw the potential of brotherhood between blacks and whites, and he now preached the equality of the races. Malcolm X reconsidered statements he had made in the past and had the courage to state, "But a person must make the effort to learn, and growing is the inevitable reward of learning."[8] He told Angelou and her friends of his plans to take the case of African Americans before the General Assembly of the United Nations, where he hoped their cause would be debated by all the world's nations. Then, America would be forced to face up to its policies of discrimination.

Malcolm X's presence in Ghana had inspired Angelou and her friends, and she was honored that he shared photographs of his wife and daughters with her. She remembered many wise statements he made, including: "Don't be in such a hurry to condemn a person because he doesn't do what you do, or think as you think or as fast. There was a time when you didn't know what you know today."[9]

When Malcolm X returned to the United States, he corresponded with Angelou and her friends. He told them of the death threats he had received and asked them to welcome some visitors he was sending. One of these friends was the talented artist Tom Feelings, who twenty years later would collaborate with Angelou on a book, entitled *Now Sheba Sings the Song*. Angelou's poetry and Feelings' art blended "to celebrate the life and beauty of black women everywhere, a beauty of the soul."[10]

Before Angelou's return to the United States, she traveled to Ghana's town of Keta which had been hard hit during the slave trade. The journey provided a startling encounter. Angelou met a woman who resembled her grandmother, the late Annie Henderson of Stamps, Arkansas, and she heard of the tragedy that had occurred in the village of Keta hundreds of years before:

> At one point every inhabitant was either killed or taken. The only escapees were children who ran away and hid in the bush. Many of them watched from their hiding places as their parents were beaten and put into chains. They saw the slaves set fire to the village. They saw mothers and fathers take infants by their feet and bash their heads against tree trunks rather than see them sold into slavery. What they saw they remembered and all that they remembered they told over and over.[11]

Maya Angelou and award-winning artist Tom Feelings at a book signing for *Now Sheba Sings the Song*. They first met in Ghana in the 1960s.

The nearby villagers took in the children of Keta. When these surviving children grew up, they rebuilt Keta and kept the story of their parents alive. The women Angelou met were descendants of those orphaned children. When these women saw Maya Angelou, who looked so much like them and whose voice sounded so much like theirs, they were sure she was a descendant of those stolen mothers and fathers of Keta. Her presence caused them to mourn for their lost people.

Angelou mourned, too, but she also felt hope in encountering her past. Despite all the centuries of suffering, her race had survived. Uprooted from their home and treated horribly in slave ships, her ancestors had carried Africa with them to America. As Angelou left Ghana willingly, in the comfort of a plane, she too carried Africa with her close to her heart.

When Angelou returned to the United States, she planned to work with Malcolm X in the newly created Organization of Afro-American Unity, but on February 21, 1965, just two days after her return, Malcolm X was assassinated in New York City. Angelou was deeply hurt by his untimely death, but she remembered his words: "You have seen Africa, bring it home and teach our people about the homeland."[12]

Soon Maya Angelou would share more of her journey outward and inward, to both teach and inspire.

9

AN ELECTRIC
DECADE

Maya Angelou once told an interviewer:

> Every human being is born with talent. It's very much like electricity. . . . It can be used to heat a house, or light up a cathedral, or put someone to death in the electric chair. It's all a question of how it's used.[1]

In the 1970s, Maya Angelou continued taking risks. She worked hard and used her talent to enrich the decade. In the late 1960s Angelou drew on her experiences in Africa to write *Black, Blues, Black,* ten one-hour programs for National Educational Television showcasing the important role of African culture in American life. She explained the meaning of the title:

"In Africa we were Blacks, brought by slavery to the U.S. Our condition of misery could be called the Blues, and now through our awareness of our African heritage, we were proudly becoming Blacks again."[2]

At social gatherings, "she often mesmerized her listeners" as she rhythmically related stories of her past.[3] Recognizing her unique ability, her friends James Baldwin and Jules and Judy Feiffer encouraged Angelou to write her life story. Judy Feiffer informed Robert Loomis, an editor at Random House, of Angelou's talent. Loomis tried to convince Angelou to write an autobiography. After she refused his offer several times, he told her, "I'm rather glad you decided not to write an autobiography because to write an autobiography as literature is the most difficult thing anyone could do."[4] When he phrased the offer as a challenge, Angelou accepted.

With the publication of *I Know Why the Caged Bird Sings* in 1970, Maya Angelou touched the hearts of millions. This critically acclaimed book's title is taken from the poem "Sympathy" by Paul Laurence Dunbar, one of Angelou's favorite poets since childhood. Many people identified with the book's theme: A person can survive in a hostile world and still emerge with courage and dignity. Angelou explained, "One must learn to care for oneself first, so that one can then dare to care for someone else. That's what it takes to make the caged bird sing."[5]

This best-seller received great praise. Editor Robert Loomis said of Angelou, "She wrote with such anger and disgust at the prejudice, but did not have any of the bitterness, which ruins a lot of writers."[6] *Life* magazine described Maya Angelou as "a dancer who writes a graceful, pirouetting style that can switch to down-home blues in about one funky second."[7] James Baldwin stated, "Her portrait is a Biblical study of life in the midst of death."[8] With her first book's success, the forty-two-year-old writer was invited to lecture at universities around the country, and she received a fellowship to Yale University.

The year 1970 was also enhanced by the literary contributions of other gifted African-American women, including Alice Walker's *The Third Life of Grange Copeland*, Toni Morrison's *The Bluest Eye*, Mari Evans's "I Am A Black Woman," and Nikki Giovanni's "Ego Tripping."

In 1973, Maya Angelou married English writer/cartoonist Paul de Feu at the multiracial Glide Community Church in San Francisco, and for a great portion of the 1970s they lived in northern California. Both loved to cook, and they shared the preparation for large dinners with family and friends. Angelou's son, Guy Johnson, whom she considered her greatest gift, continued to bring her happiness.[9] Angelou welcomed her grandson, Colin Ashanti Murphy-Johnson, into her world.

In 1974, *Gather Together in My Name*, the second volume of Angelou's autobiography, was published. This book was difficult to work on, for it contained painful parts of her past. As she debated whether she should reveal such distressing experiences, she discussed this concern with her mother, son, brother, and husband. She told them "This is what I want to do. I want to say to young people, 'You may encounter many defeats, but you must not be defeated.'"

Maya Angelou on the set of *Georgia, Georgia* in 1972 with director Stig Bjorkman (right) and actor Dirk Benedict. Angelou was the first African-American woman to have an original screenplay produced.

After hearing several chapters, her family encouraged her. "My mother said. 'Write it.' My brother said, 'Send it in.' My son got up . . . and reached over and got Paul and me in those massive arms and said, 'You're so great, Mom. Please tell it.'"[10] This book was greeted with good reviews and generous praise.

Volume three of her autobiography, *Singin' and Swingin' and Gettin' Merry Like Christmas*, the story of Angelou's stage debut and her international tour in *Porgy and Bess*, appeared two years later, and went into a second printing even before its publication date. Its special title is derived from a time in the 1920s and 1930s when African Americans would spend the time from Saturday night into Sunday evening socializing, attending church, and enjoying a Sunday meal in order to get energy to live the rest of the week.

Angelou's excellent memory enhanced the quality of the book. A reviewer wrote that the time period Angelou covered "is recalled with such astounding, bittersweet detail it borders on the surreal."[11] After the book was complete, Angelou's mother found letters Angelou had written to her during the time that she wrote about in this book; she said that her daughter had remembered people and events "exactly as they'd happened so long ago."[12]

In addition to her three well-received autobiographies published in the 1970s, three of Angelou's poetry collections were also published. Her first volume of poetry, *Just*

The Rockefeller Foundation's Bellagio Study and Conference Center on Lake Como, Italy, where Maya Angelou spent November and December 1975 as a scholar-in-residence. There she wrote a good portion of *Singin' and Swingin' and Gettin' Merry Like Christmas.*

Give Me a Cool Drink of Water 'Fore I Diiie was nominated for a Pulitzer Prize. *Oh, Pray My Wings Are Gonna Fit Me Well* was published in 1975, and her third volume of poetry, *And Still I Rise,* appeared in 1978.

A reviewer for *Publishers Weekly* praised Angelou's poems for their "human warmth, honesty, strength, and deep-rooted sense of personal pride."[13] *Contemporary Poets* reported: "She has an uncanny ability to capture the sound of a voice on a page . . . vocal, oral, and written aspects blend in her poetry."[14] Although one critic suggested that Angelou's verse is "slight" and "thin,"[15] in general critics praised Angelou's poetry for "constructing a moving record of a modern African-American woman's life,"[16] and readers all over the world appreciate her poetry. Angelou has accepted the negative reviews that occasionally come her way: "I do the best I can with everything. I have no apologies. . . . I hope I will have learned by next year to be even more total. But right now I cannot be better than I am. I'm holding nothing back."[17]

One of Maya Angelou's favorite poems, "Song for the Old Ones," appeared in her second poetry volume.[18] She explained its importance:

> A number of young blacks decided that Uncle Toms are to be laughed at and ridiculed, and I feel just the opposite. We often don't realize how those people who were scratching when they didn't itch, laughing when they weren't tickled, and saying, 'Yassuh, you sho' is right, I sho' is stupid,' we don't know how many times

their throats closed on them in pain. They did that so they could make a little money, so they could pay for somebody to go to school, to get some shoes. So that poem is for them.[19]

This is an excerpt from Angelou's "Song for the Old Ones":

They used the finest cunning
their naked wits and wiles
the lowly Uncle Tomming,
and Aunt Jemimas' smiles.

They've laughed to shield their crying
they shuffled through their dreams
and stepped 'n' fetched a country
to write the blues with screams.

I understand their meaning
it could and did derive
from living on the edge of death
They kept my race alive.[20]

In addition to writing, teaching, touring, and lecturing, Angelou earned a Tony™ award nomination for her performance in the 1973 play *Look Away* and an Emmy nomination in 1977 for her portrayal of Nyo Boto, Kunta Kinte's grandmother, in the television miniseries *Roots*, a role she modeled after her own grandmother, Annie Henderson. Even though she had achieved success in writing, people stopped her on the street, inquiring, "You're the actress in *Roots*. What's your name again, and what have you been doing all this time?"[21]

Maya Angelou with Alex Haley, author of *Roots*, and actor Levar Burton who portrayed Kunta Kinte. Angelou played Nyo Boto in the critically acclaimed television miniseries.

Angelou's successful decade as a writer required time and self-discipline. She often worked sixteen hours a day. After working most of the morning, Angelou would set aside her writing, tend her vegetable garden, take a walk, or clean the house. Later she would revise the work, often throwing most of it away. When a reviewer complimented her with the words "She's a natural writer," Angelou was upset. "A natural writer! And here I've been working maybe two weeks on a single paragraph—a paragraph that nobody's going to notice at all."[22]

By the end of this ten-year period, Angelou had co-written the teleplay for the television movie of *I Know Why the Caged Bird Sings*, the novel that had set the successful decade in motion for her. Angelou's career would continue to shine.

10

"AND STILL I RISE"

he folk singer Odetta once told Maya Angelou, "Keep on telling the truth, Maya. Stay on the stage. I don't mean the night-club stage, or the theatrical stage. I mean on the stage of life."[1]

Maya Angelou, whose ebony hair now reveals a hint of silver, has remained on the stage of life. She continues to remind us that people are more alike than unalike, that their spirit can triumph and rise over adversity. Her belief that "despite nights of terror, and fear, and pain, and grief, and disconsolation, somehow morning comes and we get up and continue on" speaks to millions, who listen because she is a survivor and an excellent writer.[2]

Described as "one of the great voices of contemporary literature,"[3] Angelou has blessed her audiences with additional volumes of her autobiography, poetry collections, children's books, screenplays, song lyrics, TV appearances, lectures, poetry readings, interviews, and acting roles in John Singleton's movie *Poetic Justice* and Jocelyn Moorhouse's *How to Make an American Quilt*.

Despite all her fame, she still remembers her beginnings as a writer, her belief that if William Shakespeare, Charles Dickens, Langston Hughes, and James Weldon Johnson could write, so could she. They inspired her to begin writing what she terms "some of the worst poetry you will ever hear of." She adds, "But at least I started trying."[4]

If the pain of her past always remains with her, so does the strength she has gained from it:

> I do think my respect for human beings comes from that period of muteness when I learned how to concentrate. I imagined my whole body as an ear and as a result I've been able to learn languages by just giving myself over to sound.[5]

Throughout Maya Angelou's life she has encountered people who "turned her suffering rage upward and brought a poet to life,"[6] including the kind and wise Bertha Flowers, who showed her the beauty of language. Angelou, who never forgot the kindnesses

Maya Angelou reading from *Now Sheba Sings the Song* in 1987.

she received along the journey, is a "Mrs. Flowers" to millions. She once said to a group of school children in Stamps, "I would love to be an encouragement . . . I hope you'll remember me. I have you in my heart. I see myself in you . . . I hope you see yourselves in me."[7]

Her son, Guy Johnson, remains a source of happiness. "If I have a monument in this world, it is my son," she says proudly. "He is a joy, a sheer delight. A good human being who belongs to himself."[8] He, too, writes poetry, and before one of his readings, he paid tribute to Angelou: "First, let me recite to you some of the poets my mother raised me on."[9]

Vivian Baxter Johnson, who had been absent in her daughter's formative years, later became a friend and an inspiration to Angelou. When she died a year before her daughter's historic Inauguration Day presentation, Angelou mourned her death. Angelou fondly remembers when she was twenty her mother praised her for having a rare combination of intelligence and kindness. "I began to set my sights higher. . . . For on that day I believed that I might just reach the top."[10]

After Angelou and Paul de Feu divorced in 1981, she decided to move to Winston-Salem, North Carolina. Angelou is now the lifetime Reynolds Professor of American Studies at Wake Forest University, which "affords her the chance to teach any subject of her choosing in the field of humanities."[11]

"When we give cheerfully and accept gratefully, everyone is blessed," said Maya Angelou in *Wouldn't Take Nothing For My Journey Now.*

Maya Angelou loves teaching. She explains:

The teacher doesn't teach, not really. The teacher offers stimulation and ways in which the person can educate himself or herself. At best the teacher wakes up, shakes up that person and makes a person hungry.[12]

Proud of her culture, Angelou often wears African-style dresses and headwraps. Her eighteen-room brick colonial home is decorated with African carvings, sculptures, and paintings by John Biggers, Phoebe, Romare Beardon, and other leading African-American artists. African music fills her sprawling house. Angelou is "aware of Africa's complex and diversified importance to world history and the role of Africa's women as its rich source of nurturing power."[13] She enjoys entertaining, and in 1994 she hosted a party at her home honoring two friends: Nobel laureate Toni Morrison and United States poet laureate Rita Dove.

Angelou continues to be involved with causes she cares about. "Once you find the truth, you ought to be prepared to stand on the street corner and use all your gifts to right the wrong."[14]

In 1988 she and friend, author Alice Walker, were arrested at an anti-apartheid rally in Berkeley, California. She recalled the African-American police officer who made the arrest: "When she fingerprinted me, her hands were shaking, and she asked me for my autograph."[15]

Angelou made a videotape against racism for the student body at Olivet College, and during the late 1980s she wrote a script on teenage parenting. In 1992, she hosted PBS's *Maya Angelou: Rainbow in the Cloud*, introducing the people of San Francisco's Glide Memorial Church, "who are leading a struggle for survival and dignity in the inner city."[16] In March 1992 she went to London to receive a special tribute by the National Society for the Prevention of Cruelty to Children, which named a new facility The Maya Angelou Child Protection Team and Family Center. In 1994, she contributed her talent to a promotional spot for the United Negro College Fund's Fiftieth Anniversary Campaign featuring a condensed version of her poem "Still I Rise":

Just like moons and like suns
—with the certainty of tides . . .
Just like hopes, springing high . . . Still I rise.
Out of the huts of history's shame, I rise.
Up from a past rooted in pain, I rise.
I'm a black ocean, leaping and wide,
welling and swelling, I bear in the tide,
Leaving behind nights of terror and fear,
I rise.
Into a daybreak, miraculously clear, I rise . . .
Bringing the gifts that my ancestors gave,
I am the hope and the dream of the slave.
And so, I rise . . . I rise . . .
I rise.[17]

Angelou often receives four hundred letters a week, and she travels around the United States making as many as eighty appearances a year, lecturing to packed houses:

Anyone who has been present at one of Angelou's readings and/or lectures knows the almost hypnotic effect she can have on an audience. Indeed, many respond to the towering (six feet plus) grandmother

Maya Angelou and distinguished artist and illustrator Tom Feelings together after one of her lectures in California.

figure almost as they would to a rock star; she performs, lectures, scolds, and teaches, providing direction and further enhancing her place.[18]

The year 1993 brought many significant moments to Angelou's life. On Wednesday, January 20, 1993, Angelou, who for a period in her life would not speak, read her inaugural poem to millions. Two days later, she was chosen as ABC-TV's Person of the Week. On

Maya Angelou and First Lady Hillary Rodham Clinton, a great admirer of Dr. Angelou, meet in August of 1994.

April 4, 1993, guests and celebrities from all over the world gathered to celebrate a two-day event marking Angelou's sixty-fifth birthday. She received greetings from President Clinton who sent her a videotape on which he called her a "treasure to the world."[19] Her party was hosted by her dear friend, Oprah Winfrey, who designed Angelou's beaded dress and arranged for a tiered cake topped with sugar flowers. Angelou said that Winfrey "is the kind of daughter I would have wanted to have."[20] Angelou dedicated her 1993 best-seller *Wouldn't Take Nothing for My Journey Now* to Winfrey, "with immeasurable love."

Although Maya Angelou has been awarded more than fifty honorary degrees, most of her lessons have been learned from life experiences. In telling us about her life, Maya Angelou helps us to understand so much about ourselves.

She writes:

> We all should know that diversity makes for a rich tapestry, and we must understand that all the threads of the tapestry are equal in value no matter their color; equal in importance no matter their texture.

> Our young must be taught that racial peculiarities do exist, but that beneath the skin, beyond the differing features and into the true heart of being, fundamentally, we are more alike, my friend, than we are unalike.[21]

CHRONOLOGY

1928—Born Marguerite Johnson on April 4, in St. Louis, Missouri.

1931—Maya with her brother, Bailey, sent to Stamps, Arkansas, to live with their grandmother, Annie Henderson.

1940—Graduates from Lafayette Training School; she and Bailey move to California to live with their mother.

1944—Works for the Market Street Railway as a trolley car conductor.

1945—Graduates from high school in San Francisco; her son, Clyde (Guy) Johnson, is born.

1952—Marries Tosh Angelos, they divorce several years later.

1953—Performs at the Purple Onion in San Francisco; begins to use the name Maya Angelou.

1954—Tours twenty-two nations with the touring company of
-1955 *Porgy and Bess.*

1957—Appears in an off-Broadway play, *Calypso Heat Wave*; records *Miss Calypso*, an album for Liberty Records.

1959—Moves to New York with Guy and joins the Harlem Writers Guild.

1960—Organizes *Cabaret for Freedom* with Godfrey Cambridge; succeeds Bayard Rustin as northern coordinator for the Southern Christian Leadership Conference; marries Vasumzi Make; performs in the off-Broadway play *The Blacks.*

1961—Moves to Cairo, Egypt, with Make and Guy.

1962—Moves to Ghana after ending marriage with Make.

1963—Serves as assistant administrator at the University of
-1965 Ghana's School of Music and Drama at the Institute of African Studies.

1968—Writes *Black, Blues, Black* for National Educational Television.

1970—The first volume of her autobiography, *I Know Why the Caged Bird Sings,* is published.

1971—*Just Give Me a Cool Drink of Water 'Fore I Diiie,* her first volume of poetry, is published.

1972—Writes the screenplay for *Georgia, Georgia.*

1973—Nominated for a Tony™ Award in the category of Actress, Supporting or Featured (Dramatic) for the play *Look Away*; marries Paul De Feu. They divorce several years later.

1974—*Gather Together in My Name,* the second volume of her autobiography, is published.

1975—*Oh Pray My Wings Are Gonna Fit Me Well* (poetry) is published; selected as a Rockefeller Foundation Scholar in Italy.

1976—*Singin' and Swingin' and Gettin' Merry Like Christmas,* the third volume of her autobiography, is published.

1977—Plays Kunte Kinte's grandmother in Alex Haley's TV miniseries *Roots.*

1978—*And Still I Rise* (poetry) is published.

1979—Television version of *I Know Why the Caged Bird Sings* premieres on CBS.

1981—*The Heart of a Woman,* the fourth volume of her autobiography, is published.

1982—Appointed the Reynolds Chair in American Studies at Wake Forest University in Winston-Salem, North Carolina; *Sister, Sister* premieres on NBC.

1983—*Shaker, Why Don't You Sing?* (poetry) is published.

1986—*All God's Children Need Traveling Shoes,* the fifth volume of her autobiography; and *Now Sheba Sings the Song,* with artist Tom Feelings, are published.

1990—*I Shall Not Be Moved* (poetry) is published.

1992—Selected by President-elect Bill Clinton to compose a poem for his inauguration; hosts PBS: *Maya Angelou: Rainbow in the Cloud*; her play *And Still I Rise* premieres in Winston-Salem, North Carolina.

1993—Delivers her inaugural poem, "On the Pulse of Morning," to the nation; chosen ABC-TV's Person of the Week, on January 22; *Wouldn't Take Nothing for My Journey Now* is published; contributes poetry to the film *Poetic Justice*, and plays minor role in the film.

1994—*My Painted House, My Friendly Chicken and Me* and *The Complete Collected Poems of Maya Angelou* are published; she is featured in United Negro College Fund's Fiftieth Anniversary Campaign; becomes the 79th recipient of the Spingarn Medal, the highest honor the NAACP awards an individual.

1995—*Phenomenal Woman: Four Poems Celebrating Women* is published; read "A Brave and Startling Truth" at the fiftieth anniversary of the founding of the United Nations; delivers a poem at the Million Man March; receives TransAfrica Forum's Arthur R. Ashe, Jr., Humanitarian Award; is presented with Frank G. Wells Award at the American Teacher Awards ceremony.

CHAPTER NOTES

Chapter 1

1. Esther Hill, "Maya Angelou: Resolving the Past, Embracing the Future," *The Student* (student literary magazine, Wake Forest University, Winston-Salem, North Carolina), Spring 1981, p. 8.

2. Maya Angelou, *I Know Why the Caged Bird Sings* (New York: Random House, 1969), p. 168.

3. Jeffrey M. Elliot, *Conversations with Maya Angelou* (Jackson, Miss.: University Press of Mississippi, 1989), p. 112.

4. Angelou, *I Know Why the Caged Bird Sings*, p. 15.

5. Howard G. Chau-Eoan and Nina Burleigh, "Moment of Creation," *People Magazine*, January 18, 1993, p. 62.

6. Ibid.

7. Karima Haynes, "Maya Angelou: Prime Time Poet," *Ebony*, April 1993, p. 72.

8. Susan Cahill, ed., *Writing Women's Lives: An Anthology of Autobiographical Narratives by Twentieth-Century American Women Writers* (New York: Harper Perennial, 1994), p. 210.

9. Elliot, p. 192.

10. Angelou, *I Know Why the Caged Bird Sings*, p. 95.

11. Maya Angelou, *The Complete Collected Poems of Maya Angelou* (New York: Random House, 1994), p. 270.

12. Haynes, p. 68.

13. Angelou, *Collected Poems*, p. 270.

14. Ibid., p. 271.

15. Ibid., p. 272.

16. Ibid.

17. Ibid.

18. Ibid., p. 273.

19. Judith Graham, ed., *Current Biography* (New York: H. W. Wilson), February 1994, Vol. 55, no. 2, p. 10.

20. Angelou, *Collected Poems*, p. 273.

21. Haynes, p. 70.

22. ABC News live broadcast of President William Jefferson Clinton's inauguration, January 20, 1993.

23. "Oprah Throws a Party," *Ebony*, June 1993, p. 120.

24. *Creativity with Bill Moyers: Maya Angelou.* Corporation for Entertainment and Learning, WNET Theater, 1982. Videotape.

Chapter 2

1. Jeffrey Elliot, *Conversations with Maya Angelou* (Jackson, Miss.: University Press of Mississippi, 1989), p. 4.

2. Maya Angelou, *I Know Why the Caged Bird Sings* (New York: Random House, 1969) p. 27.

3. Ibid., p. 7.

4. Jeffrey Elliot, "Author Maya Angelou Raps," *Sepia*, October 1977, p. 22.

5. Angelou, p. 4.

6. Ibid., pp. 4–5.

7. Ibid., p. 24.

8. *Creativity with Bill Moyers: Maya Angelou.* Corporation for Entertainment and Learning, WNET Theater, 1982. Videotape.

9. Angelou, pp. 11, 14–15.

10. *Creativity with Bill Moyers.*

11. *African-Americans: Voices of Triumph: Creative Fire* (Alexandria, Va.: Time-Life Books, 1994), p. 72.

12. Elliot, "Author Maya Angelou Raps," p. 22.

13. Angelou, p. 51.

14. Ibid., p. 53.

15. Ibid., p. 55.

16. Ibid., p. 56.

17. Ibid., p. 57.

18. Ibid., p. 58.

19. Ibid.

20. Ibid., p. 59.

21. Ibid., p. 70.

22. Ibid.

23. Ibid., p. 72.

24. Ibid., p. 76.

25. Ibid., p. 79.

26. Ibid., p. 82.

27. Personal Diary, Black Entertainment Video 1990, Schomburg Center for Research in Black Culture.

28. Angelou, p. 84.

29. Ibid., pp. 84–85.

30. Ibid., p. 85.

Chapter 3

1. William Shakespeare, *The Sonnets of William Shakespeare, Sonnet 29* (New York: Crown Publishers, 1961), p. 16.

2. *Creativity with Bill Moyers: Maya Angelou,* Corporation for Entertainment and Learning, WNET Theater, 1982 (videotape).

3. Ibid.

4. Maya Angelou, *I Know Why the Caged Bird Sings* (New York: Random House, 1969), p. 98.

5. *Creativity with Bill Moyers.*

6. Ibid.

7. Angelou, *I Know Why the Caged Bird Sings,* pp. 91–92.

8. Lawrence Toppman, "Maya Angelou: The Serene Spirit of a Survivor," *Charlotte Observer*, December 11, 1983, p. 1.

9. Jeffrey Elliot, *Conversations with Maya Angelou* (Jackson, Miss.: University Press of Mississippi, 1989), p. 73.

10. Esther Hill, "Maya Angelou: Resolving the Past, Embracing the Future," *The Student* (student literary magazine, Wake Forest University, Winston-Salem, North Carolina), Spring 1981, pp. 7–8.

11. Catherine S. Manegold, "A Wordsmith at Her Inaugural Anvil," *New York Times*, Jan. 20, 1993, p. C8.

12. Angelou, *I Know Why the Caged Bird Sings,* pp. 131, 132.

13. Ibid., p. 167.

14. Ibid., p. 169.

15. Ibid., p. 170.

16. Edgar Allan Poe, "Annabel Lee," stanza 5. *A Treasury of the World's Best-Loved Poems* (New York: Avenel Books, 1961), p. 138.

17. Angelou, *I Know Why the Caged Bird Sings,* pp. 174–175.

18. Ibid., pp. 175–176.
19. Ibid., p. 176.
20. Ibid., p. 178.
21. Ibid., p. 179.
22. Ibid.
23. Ibid., p. 184.
24. Maya Angelou, *Gather Together in My Name* (New York: Random House, 1974), p. 64.
25. Ibid., p. 77.
26. Toppman, p. 1.

Chapter 4

1. Maya Angelou, *I Know Why the Caged Bird Sings* (New York: Random House, 1969) p. 198.
2. Ibid., p. 201.
3. Ibid., p. 206.
4. Ibid., p. 204.
5. Ibid., p. 207.
6. Ibid., p. 209.
7. Ibid., pp. 210–211.
8. Maya Angelou, *Gather Together in My Name* (New York: Random House, 1974), p. 55.
9. Angelou, *I Know Why the Caged Bird Sings*, p. 223.
10. Ibid., p. 240.
11. Ibid., p. 247.
12. Ibid., p. 256.
13. Ibid., p. 258.
14. Ibid., p. 260.
15. Ibid., p. 261.
16. Ibid., p. 262.
17. Ibid., pp. 262–263.
18. Ibid., p. 263.
19. Ibid., pp. 265, 272.
20. Ibid., pp. 272–273.
21. Ibid., p. 276.
22. Ibid., pp. 276–277.
23. Ibid., p. 279.
24. Ibid., p. 280.

25. Ibid., p. 281.

Chapter 5

1. Maya Angelou, *Gather Together in My Name* (New York: Random House, 1974) pp. 5, 7–8.

2. Walter Blum, "Listening to Maya Angelou," California Living, *San Francisco Examiner*, December 14, 1975, p. 12.

3. Angelou, p. 14.

4. Ibid., p. 26.

5. Ibid., p. 27.

6. Ibid.

7. Ibid., p. 66.

8. Ibid., p. 70.

9. Ibid., p. 73.

10. Ibid., p. 90.

11. Ibid., pp. 92–93.

12. Ibid., p. 93.

13. Ibid.

14. Ibid., p. 94.

15. Ibid., p. 99.

16. Ibid., p. 107.

17. Ibid., p. 109.

18. Ibid., p. 137.

19. Ibid., pp. 137–138.

20. Ibid., p. 144.

21. Ibid., p. 189.

22. Ibid., p. 171.

23. Ibid., p. 180.

24. Ibid., p. 188.

25. Ibid., p. 201.

26. Ibid., pp. 205–206.

27. Ibid., p. 208.

28. Ibid., p. 213.

29. Ibid., p. 214.

Chapter 6

1. Maya Angelou, *Singin' and Swingin' and Gettin' Merry Like Christmas* (New York: Random House, 1976), p. 3.

2. Jeffrey Elliot, *Conversations with Maya Angelou* (Jackson, Miss.: University Press of Mississippi, 1989), p. 30.

3. Angelou, *Singin' and Swingin' and Gettin' Merry Like Christmas*, p. 32.

4. Ibid., p. 48.

5. Ibid., p. 100.

6. Ibid., p. 108.

7. Ibid., p. 127.

8. Ibid., pp. 143–144.

9. Ibid., p. 157.

10. Maya Angelou, *Wouldn't Take Nothing for My Journey Now* (New York: Random House, 1993), p. 12.

11. Angelou, *Singin' and Swingin' and Gettin' Merry Like Christmas*, pp. 253–254.

12. Ibid., pp. 257–258.

13. Ibid., p. 258.

14. Ibid., p. 259.

15. Ibid., pp. 258–259.

16. Ibid., p. 262.

17. Ibid., pp. 262–263.

18. Ibid., p. 267.

Chapter 7

1. Maya Angelou, *The Heart of a Woman* (New York: Random House, 1981), p. 21.

2. Ibid., p. 22.

3. Ibid., p. 38.

4. Ibid., p. 39.

5. Ibid., p. 40.

6. Ibid., p. 43.

7. Ibid., p. 48.

8. Ibid., p. 50.

9. Jeffrey Elliot, "Author Maya Angelou Raps," *Sepia*, October 1977, p. 27.

10. Angelou, pp. 97–98.

11. Ibid., p. 102.

12. Ibid., p. 179.

13. Ibid., p. 174.

14. Ibid., p. 179.

15. Ibid., p. 141.

16. Ibid., p. 142.

17. Ibid., pp. 185–186.

18. Ibid., p. 191.

19. Ibid., pp. 211–213.

20. Ibid., p. 233.

21 Maya Angelou, *All God's Children Need Traveling Shoes* (New York: Random House, 1986), pp. 151–152.

22. Angelou, *The Heart of a Woman*, p. 257.

23. Ibid.

24. Russell Harris, "Zelo Interviews Maya Angelou," *Zelo*, Fall 1986, p. 66.

Chapter 8

1. Maya Angelou, *All God's Children Need Traveling Shoes* (New York: Random House, 1986), p. 185.

2. Ibid., p. 17.

3. Ibid., p. 29.

4. Ibid., p. 3.

5. Ibid., p. 20.

6. Ibid., p. 58.

7. Ibid., p. 125.

8. Ibid., p. 130.

9. Ibid., p. 145.

10. Joseph Harper, review of *Now Sheba Sings the Song* by Maya Angelou, illustrated by Tom Feelings, *School Library Journal*, October 1987, pp. 146–147.

11. Angelou, p. 206.

12. Ibid., p. 139.

Chapter 9

1. Jeffrey Elliot, "Author Maya Angelou Raps," *Sepia*, October 1977, p. 27.

2. Maya Angelou, "Why I Moved Back to the South," *Ebony* February, 1982, p. 133.

3. Judith Graham, ed., *Current Biography* (New York: H. W. Wilson), February 1994, vol. 55, no. 2, p. 9.

4. Claudia Tate, ed., *Black American Women Writers at Work* (New York: Continuum, 1983), p. 6.

5. Elliot, p. 27.

6. Greg Hilt, "Maya Angelou," *Winston-Salem Journal*, December 6, 1987, p. A16.

7. *Life*, June 5, 1970, vol. 68, no. 21, p. 12.

8. Nancy Shuker, *Maya Angelou* (Englewood Cliffs, N.J.: Silver Burdett, 1990), p. 112.

9. Stephanie Stokes Oliver, "Maya Angelou: The Heart of a Woman," *Essence*, May 1983, p. 114.

10. Carol Benson, "Interview with Maya Angelou," *Writers Digest*, January 1975, vol. 55, no. 1, p. 19.

11. Beth Ann Krier, "Maya Angelou: No Longer a Caged Bird," *Los Angeles Times*, September 24, 1976, IV, p. 1.

12. Jeffrey Elliot, *Conversations with Maya Angelou* (Jackson, Miss.: University Press of Mississippi, 1989), p. 80.

13. Graham, pp. 9–10.

14. James Vinson and D. L. Kirkpatrick, *Contemporary Poets*, 4th ed. (New York: St. Martins Press, 1985), p. 17.

15. Graham, p. 10.

16. Ibid.

17. Walter Blum, "Listening to Maya Angelou," California Living, *San Francisco Examiner*, December 14, 1975, p. 23.

18. Ibid., p. 22.

19. Ibid.

20. Maya Angelou, *The Complete Collected Poems of Maya Angelou* (New York: Random House, 1994), pp. 108–109.

21. Jeffrey Elliot, *Conversations with Maya Angelou*, p. 71.

22. Blum, p. 16.

Chapter 10

1. Maya Angelou, *The Heart of a Woman* (New York: Random House, 1981), p. 74.

2. Karima Haynes, "Maya Angelou: Prime Time Poet," *Ebony*, April 1993, p. 72.

⊡⊡⊡⊡⊡⊡⊡⊡⊡⊡⊡⊡⊡⊡⊡⊡⊡⊡⊡⊡⊡⊡⊡⊡⊡⊡⊡⊡⊡⊡⊡⊡⊡⊡

3. *Books for Young Readers Catalogue* (New York: Crown Publishers, Fall 1994), p. 19.

4. *The Entertainers: Program 3*, *Ebony/Jet* Guide to Black Excellence, Johnson-Conrad Productions, 1991 (videotape).

5. Jeffrey Elliot, *Conversations with Maya Angelou* (Jackson, Miss.: University Press of Mississippi, 1989), p. 203.

6. *Creativity with Bill Moyers: Maya Angelou*, Corporation for Entertainment and Learning, WNET Theater, 1982 (videotape).

7. Ibid.

8. Elliot, p. 203.

9. Mary Chamberlain, ed., *Writing Lives: Conversations Between Women Writers* (London: Virago Press), p. 9.

10. *Ebony*, May 1993, vol. XLVIII, no. 7, p. 32.

11. Russell Harris, "Zelo Interviews Maya Angelou," *Zelo*, Fall 1986, p. 64.

12. Ibid., p. 67.

13. Maya Angelou, *Now Sheba Sings the Song*, illustrated by Tom Feelings. (New York: E. P. Dutton/Dial Books, 1987), Introduction–p. 5.

14. Sal Manna, "The West Interview: Maya Angelou," *San Jose Mercury News*, June 22, 1986, p. 4.

15. Judith Graham, ed., *Current Biography* (New York: H. W. Wilson), February 1994, vol. 55, no. 2, p. 11.

16. *Essence*, May 1992, vol. 23, p. 68.

17. Maya Angelou, "Still I Rise," public service announcement for United Negro College Fund, Advertising Council, Inc., 1994.

18. Elaine Showalter, *Modern American Women Writers* (New York: Charles Scribner's Sons, 1991), p. 7.

19. "Oprah Throws a Party," *Ebony*, June 1993, p. 120.

20. Ibid.

21. Maya Angelou, *Wouldn't Take Nothing for My Journey Now* (New York: Random House, 1993), p. 124.

FURTHER READING

Books

Angelou, Maya. *All God's Children Need Traveling Shoes.* New York: Random House, 1986.

———. *The Complete Collected Poems of Maya Angelou.* New York: Random House, 1994.

———. *Gather Together in My Name.* New York: Random House, 1974.

———. *The Heart of a Woman.* New York: Random House, 1981.

———. *I Know Why the Caged Bird Sings.* New York: Random House, 1969.

———. *Life Doesn't Frighten Me.* New York: Stewart, Tabori, and Chang, 1993.

———. *My Painted House, My Friendly Chicken, and Me.* New York: Crown, 1994.

———. *Now Sheba Sings the Song.* New York: E. P. Dutton, 1987.

———. *On the Pulse of Morning.* New York: Random House, 1993.

———. *Phenomenal Woman: Four Poems Celebrating Women.* New York: Random House, 1995.

———. *Singin' and Swingin' and Gettin' Merry Like Christmas.* New York: Random House, 1976.

———. *Wouldn't Take Nothing for My Journey Now.* New York: Random House, 1993.

Elliot, Jeffrey M., ed. *Conversations with Maya Angelou.* Jackson, Miss.: University of Mississippi Press, 1989.

King, Sarah. *Maya Angelou: Greeting the Morning.* Brookfield, Conn.: Millbrook Press, 1994.

Shapiro, Miles. *Maya Angelou: Author.* New York: Chelsea House, 1994.

Shuker, Nancy. *Maya Angelou.* Englewood Cliffs, N.J.: Silver Burdett, 1990.

Audiotapes

On the Pulse of Morning. Random House, 1993.

Wouldn't Take Nothing For My Journey Now. Random House, 1993.

Videotapes

Creativity with Bill Moyers: Maya Angelou. Corporation for Entertainment and Learning, WNET Theater, 1982.

The Entertainers: Program 3. Ebony/Jet Guide to Black Excellence, Johnson-Conrad Productions, 1991.

Personal Diary featuring an interview with Maya Angelou. Host, Ed Gordon. Black Entertainment Television, 1990. Schomberg Center for Research in Black Culture, 515 Lenox Avenue, New York, NY 10037-1801.

Rainbow in the Clouds. Maya Angelou at Glide Memorial Church in San Francisco, PBS, 1992.

INDEX